ALEC GUINNESS

ALEC GUINNESS

A CELEBRATION

JOHN RUSSELL TAYLOR

PAVILION

For Y.Y.L.

This edition published in Great Britain in 2000 by
PAVILION BOOKS LIMITED
London House, Great Eastern Wharf
Parkgate Road, London SW11 4NQ
www.pavilionbooks.co.uk

First edition published in 1984 by
Pavilion Books Limited

A CIP catalogue record for this book is available
from the British Library.

ISBN 1 86205 501 7

Printed in Spain by Bookprint

10 9 8 7 6 5 4 3 2 1

This book can be ordered direct from the publisher.
Please contact the Marketing Department.
But try your bookshop first.

CONTENTS

When Alec Guinness died, on 5 August 2000, a mere ten weeks before Merula, his wife of sixty-two years, the sheer outpourng of affection was amazing. It was not, of course, astonishing that the event should occasion a lot of comment: Guinness was, after all, the last of an heroic generation of English actors, and if semi-retired was still prominent enough in the public eye to be regarded as current. Naturally, most of those reminiscing about him were talking mainly about the past – that, after all, is the definition of reminiscence – but seldom the far distant past. Indeed, Guinness seemed to be remembered primarily for his roles in *Star Wars* (with its sequels) and *Tinker, Tailor, Soldier, Spy* (with its sequel), all of them made since 1977. Any child, practically, could have seen those, and in the case of *Star Wars*, a lot of them did. It was interesting to compare the obituaries with those of John Gielgud, who was ten years older than Guinness, and died only a few months earlier.

With Gielgud the keynote was respect – almost reverence – and measured yet enthusiastic judgement: he had become, though still acting at ninety-seven, a monument rather than a person, and ironically the only really personal element in all the encomia was the opportunity his death offered to go back and discuss in detail the homosexual scandal in the Forties that might have blighted his career, but in the event did not. With Guinness the tone was quite different: it was affectionate.

This was surprising. But why should it have been? Guinness was, certainly, a huge star. But more important to public reputation, he was very definitely a film star too. Film stars we see in close-up; we feel physically close to them, and that somehow betokens emotional involvement as well. Not necessarily liking: there has always been the sort of star who positively revels in being 'the man (or woman) you love to hate'. But Guinness was, by general agreement, not the sort of star that you automatically cosy up to, nor did you ever, really, love to hate him. So why the affection?

I must, I suppose, be typical of my generation in that my first awareness of Alec Guinness came through *Great Expectations*. In a crowded gallery of grotesques, it seemed unlikely that Herbert Pocket, that thankless character in any film, the hero's best friend, should stand out. Moreover, this young actor (not so young as he appeared, but still...) had never made a film before, if we except a solitary experience as an extra some thirteen years earlier, and I was much too young to realise that he had had a career of promise, even distinction, in the theatre in that faraway time before the War. So why should this apparently unprepossessing actor, in an unrewarding role, remain lodged in my consciousness? It certainly was not through backing into the limelight: there were no unfair actor's tricks to grab attention where it was not due. Almost the reverse, in fact. The very intensity and single-mindedness of the actor's absorption in his role, I now think, his determination to disappear completely within it, somehow singled him out: it was a memorable performance because

OPPOSITE: Alec Guinness in 1952 by Cecil Beaton.

it seemed not to be a performance at all.

The next significant step in my acquaintance with Guinness was *Kind Hearts and Coronets* – much more than his Fagin, which came in between. *Kind Hearts and Coronets*, of course, was an actor's tour-de-force, immediately recognisable as such. No one is going to play eight different members of a family without immediately being labelled 'man of a thousand faces'. Easy to say, too, that such a performance is a triumph of makeup rather than acting art. Some did say that, and yet again what was really striking about the performance was the actor's complete immersion in the role(s): however caricatured the ebullient suffragette or the bloodthirsty general might seem, one believed in them because they were completely true to their own inner reality, with no hint that anyone was expected to recognise the same actor in different disguises – least of all, the actor himself.

That may be all very well for one film, or for a long career as a respectable character actor, one of those you vaguely recognise without ever being altogether sure of the name. But Guinness was evidently not going to fall into that sort of category. He was going to be a star, but of a very special kind, or so it seemed. Finally, though, there is no special kind of star, only the stars and the rest. A star, a true star, always builds on his or her own personality, and the effect of transformation from role to role is strictly relative: how different are they from what we expect them to be, how ingenious can the variations be without rendering the basic theme unrecognisable? So if Guinness was really a star, we have to recognise a consistent personality, the theme on which the variations are based.

So what is it that held audiences in thrall from *The Bridge on the River Kwai* to *Tinker, Tailor, Soldier, Spy*? Katharine Hepburn says of actors she approves of 'He has a secret'. Meaning, no doubt, not a literal secret, or even a secret of technique, but a hidden source of power, an inherent mystery which, like The Force in *Star Wars*, its owner no doubt does not fully comprehend, and cannot, even if he wishes to, escape. Alec Guinness was just such a sphinx. Maybe in his own estimation a sphinx without a secret, someone whose extraordinary quality resided in his very ordinariness, his lack of distinguishing features. Certainly I know sensible people, well versed in show business, who have met Guinness socially, been casually introduced by Christian name, and absolutely not realized who he was. But that, of course, is life; the screen or the stage is a very different matter.

Russell Davies, reviewing the second television series featuring John Le Carré's master secret agent George Smiley in 1982, made a mischievous but not totally frivolous suggestion:

'Guinness himself has spoken of "The art of doing nothing", and it's an art he has been refining for some time. In 1959 Noël Coward in his journal, remarked of *Our Man In Havana*: "Alec! well, I'm a bit puzzled. He is a beautiful actor but, to my mind, he plays the whole thing in too minor a key. It is a faultless performance but actually, I'm afraid, a little dull."

'By developing this fault, Sir Alec has turned it to his advantage. Dullness is now his speciality. He has cultivated a zombie-like equilibrium – heavy on the librium – that hints, without having to say anything, at a religious depth…'

The quality of being interesting because you are so transcendingly boring? It sounds like a neat trick to pull, if you can. Certainly Guinness's popularity had little or nothing to do with his being forthcoming, making himself appealing. There was nearly always something austere and even forbidding about the characters he played; at the very least they were wrapped up in their own fantasies of themselves, and not inclined, or not able, to let themselves be totally known. It is a true mark of Guinness's individuality that he never softened this, never asked for sympathy, either for the character or for himself, the actor peeping out from behind the role. Somewhere he must have learnt very well the lesson of 'If you want them to run after you, just walk the other way.'

To do that, to have the courage to do that, you have to be very simple or very confident. No one, to my knowledge, had ever suspected Guinness of being very simple. In his own quiet way he seemed to be thoroughly secure. Not pushily, self-assertively so, but confident that he could do anything he set out to do. Whatever he might say about his own self-doubts, his constant belief that he had made a mess of things, there was a kind of invulnerability about him which created confidence around him. Even in his eighties, Guinness remained still surprisingly unknowable. And yet known and delighted in by millions. One sometimes wonders if the real Alec Guinness knew who the real Alec Guinness was. Perhaps his great strength was that he just did not care.

So the question remains, why the affection? Why should we care at all for someone who apparently does not care for us, does not seem in what he does to give any noticeable consideration for how we may feel about it or him? Masochism might be one explanation, but masochism does not get us very far. More likely, the genuine affection people clearly feel for Guinness must come from something deeper and more instinctive: a sense that whatever façade he presents, it is only a façade from behind which a caring, involved, and probably very complex person is unconsciously signalling. I find myself reminded of another actor about whom I have written a book: Vivien Leigh. Her great, individual quality, it always seemed to me, was her absolute refusal in performance to solicit our sympathy for the characters she played. Her Scarlett O'Hara or her Blanche Dubois were what they were, careless, or unaware of how we might judge them. They might well have been not very nice people, not admirable, not the sort of person one would in real life have taken to one's bosom. Well, so be it: if we were going anyway to sympathise and try to understand, that was entirely up to us. It certainly had nothing to do with Leigh, the actress, signalling her likeability from behind the persona. Since Leigh's death, of course, we have found out much more about her private struggles with illness, physical and mental, than we were ever allowed to know at the time. But that does not alter our evaluation of the performances one way or another, though it may confirm that our original instincts were correct.

With Guinness one suspects that something of the same pattern of creativity applies. Leigh, of course, was a contemporary of Guinness, just a year older, but the whole of her career was lived in the days before the media insisted that a public person's private life could not be kept private. In Guinness's case things have been slightly different. He often stated that he was not personally shy, had no problems in communicating what he wanted, when he wanted. On the other hand, he was certainly in many ways devious, teasing, fiercely defensive of his own privacy, as far as that was possible. However, in our own media-led age total personal anonymity for a high profile actor was not possible, and little by little information about Guinness's early life began to filter through. With it came the opportunity to hypothesize about the biographical roots of his art. As long as his mother was alive (she seems to have died in 1985, when she would have been 98), he could reasonably refuse to go into any detail about his illegitimate birth, though he had disclosed it to determined American interviewers a few years earlier. He explained more about his parentage, and his search for confirmation of his father's identity, in his autobiographical volumes, starting with *Blessings in Disguise*, published in the year of his mother's death. Also belatedly revealed was his stepfather's occasionally brutal behaviour towards him. Clearly there was every reason for him to be secretive.

What was unique about him was the ability to use all this in his art. Or rather, perhaps, his inability not to use it. It was frequently said that on screen he had no personality of his own, lost completely in the role he was playing. There were certainly roles where his apparent ability to transform himself was prominent, but there was, as there had to be, always some elusive sense of a personal consistency behind the diversity. The consistency, finally, of a buried but perhaps telepathically communicated sense of hurt. Anyone receptive to the natural, inevitable telepathy between actor and audience can respond to that. And that, I believe, was what brought him genuine affection: without a sense, however obscure, that there were hidden depths, personal devils to be wrestled with, decorum that must be maintained at no matter what cost, Guinness would have been just another character actor.

Character actors command their own forms of affection, but the overwhelming sense at Guinness's death that, whatever his reserve, he belonged to us, marked him out as someone to be loved. The feeling was all the more intense because love was the last thing he ever seemed to ask for.

FIRST STEPS

Happy the land, they say, that has no history. Happy perhaps also the man: but it is difficult to be so sure. For when we come down to it really no one has no history, and the events of a life are absolutely unpredictable in terms of their effect: we all know those vulnerable ones, the 'extra pain sufferers' of an ad-man's fancy, who feel every tremble as a cataclysm and every storm in a teacup as a tidal wave. Even those who seem, eventually, to have found a certain peace and order in their lives may still retain terrible insecurities and inhibitions derived from early experiences which they claim to have forgotten or have chosen, at who knows what cost, to forget.

Sir Alec Guinness, might well have seemed cool, established, invulnerable. And yet he was the first to confess to terrible spasms of nervous tension before going on stage, to a total lack of confidence that he was doing right in a role, which often drove him to beg to be released from commitments and left him generally convinced afterwards that he had made a botch of it. Modest and self-effacing he usually was, avoiding whenever possible the first person in conversation ('One does keep on saying "one", I am afraid, but to say "I" always seems terribly pushy, don't you think?'). His private life was kept, well, rigorously private, but seemed to have been tranquil for many years – happily married to the same wife for nearly half a century, father and then grandfather; a questing youth which found many necessary answers in middle age with reception into the Roman Catholic church. The assumption always made about him which he vigorously denied was that he was shy: he could clearly communicate all he wished to with his fellow man, and when he appeared withdrawn it was because he had chosen to withdraw himself, not because he had no choice in the matter.

And yet…one cannot help noticing that few of his more memorable roles were of happy, unthinking extroverts – or even of tortured, thinking extroverts like Dylan Thomas. He was always at his best projecting existential unease, the vulnerability behind the most glacial façade, the character whose main drive in life is a constantly frustrated search for himself. Guinness might have objected all he liked to the publicity-fostered image of him as a 'man of a thousand faces', and even more as a 'man with no face'. But it does seem that the urge to discover the real him, the one face behind the many, was throughout his life a driving force; it is as though, even while he insisted that he had a face, and a very distinctive one, deep down he still wondered what he was going to see in the mirror each morning. Insecurities of the kind are generally rooted deep, and it must almost certainly be back to Guinness's rather obscure and mysterious childhood that we must go to find some kind of explanation.

The mystery starts, appropriately enough, with his birth. He always said it took place on 2 April, 1914, in Marylebone or Maida Vale. But since he was, as he once or twice indicated to determined American interviewers, illegitimate, the surname on his birth certificate remained elusive. In fact, he was born in North Paddington, and

PREVIOUS PAGE: as Osric in Gielgud's 1934 Hamlet.

his mother's name was Agnes de Cuffe; his baptismal names were Alec (so that is not short for anything) Guinness. The father of Alec Guinness de Cuffe (or simply Cuffe, as he gives it later on his marriage license) is left unnamed; all Guinness could remember, from meeting him four or five times, was that he was Scottish, handsome, white-haired – sixty-four at the time of the boy's birth – a banker named Andrew Geddes. 'I was taught to call him uncle, but I suppose I always knew he was my father.' Beyond that, all was guesswork. Guinness says that he was conceived, apparently, as the result of an indiscretion during Cowes Week, 1913, where his mother was a barmaid, and possibly part-time call-girl, on the Guinness family yacht. In any case, it seems that his father, whoever he was (not, according to belated blood tests, a Guinness) had money, and a certain amount of it came the way of Agnes and young Alec in the next few years: enough at least to keep them in a state of shabby gentility, moving, as it seems, more or less aimlessly from boarding house to boarding house along the more agreeable stretches of the south coast, starting with the Isle of Wight.

In this pattern of life, rather like something from the novels of Patrick Hamilton or, later, William Trevor (the mature Guinness never, sadly enough, appeared in an adaptation of either), young Alec was, it would seem, a quiet, well-behaved, rather solitary observer. His mother married when he was five, to a soldier called Stiven, who seems later on to have treated him on occasion quite brutally, but he generally claimed his life had no memorable incidents until he was sent off to a boarding school called Pembroke Lodge, Southbourne, at the age of six: his father had apparently set up a fund for his education. He pictured himself there as odd and, the worst possible oddity, no good at sports. He tended to get teased, but does not seem to have been unduly perturbed: by the age of seven he had discovered in himself a talent for mimicry and dramatic narration. Mainly it was during a year he had off school with a serious bout of colitis, and its aftermath. That was at Bexhill, and he spent quite a bit of his convalescence building and playing with model theatres, acting out all the roles in his imaginary dramas himself. When he got back to school he put his solitary discoveries to use, and rapidly became the dormitory story-teller, decorating his narratives with all sorts of different voices and even a flashlight which he would flash on and off for dramatic emphasis.

This made him not only a character, but an interesting character, and therefore ensured him a measure of popularity with the other boys, even if he believed he had a tendency to outstay his welcome, and be still inventing and enacting after everyone else had fallen asleep. He was in every other respect, according to his own report, entirely unprepossessing. When he took it into his head to audition for the school dramatic society he was turned down by the headmaster, who sadly assured him he would never make an actor. At the age of twelve he went on to Roborough, a private school near Eastbourne, which at least had something closer to what one might call a dramatic tradition. Unfortunately it was primarily devoted to Gilbert and Sullivan, and Guinness, though throughout his life passionately devoted to music as a listener, could never at any stage contrive to sing in tune. This tiresome disability gave further colour to the reiterated assertion that he would never make an actor, for what good were you in a nest of budding Savoyards if you could not carry a tune?

However, it was at Roborough that Guinness made his actual debut on the boards. As a change from Gilbert and Sullivan, the dramatic society was doing *Macbeth*, and he was given the brief and unremarkable role of a messenger, on the principle that though he was bound to mess it up, he could not mess it up too much. This was, to him, his big chance, and he went about the preparation of the role with what, with hindsight, we can see as characteristic care and meticulous attention to detail. He first of all firmly memorised the brief speech, and then set himself to consider how he could best create the illusion of having rushed hotfoot from the battlefield to deliver his message. No unconscious exponent of the Method he, even at that early stage: more prosaically, he decided that something like the actuality was preferable to any artful illusion so, after precisely timing the scene preceding his entrance, at the performance itself he sneaked out and stationed himself in the dark at the other end of the playing fields. When the time was ripe he set off in a pell-mell sprint back, into the school hall and on to the stage right on cue, giving an amazing impersonation of breathlessness and near physical collapse because it was no impersonation but the real thing. Flabbergasted, the audience gave the messenger a spontaneous round of applause. And, quite possibly, at that moment the die of young Alec's future was cast.

Otherwise, the skinny lad grew up into a skinny young man seeking, and receiving, no particular note from his peers. Whenever he could he went to the nearest available professional theatre, the Devonshire Theatre, Eastbourne. Academically his work was more than respectable, and he always ended up, if never showily at the top of his class, then at least respectably close to it. Particularly in English, thereby encouraging his alternative ambitions to become a writer. When he left school at the age of seventeen, he still had a small allowance from his educational fund, of twenty-six shillings (£1.30) a week, which in 1932 was not the derisory sum it now sounds, but still was not possible to live reasonably on. Obviously he had to find a job: drawing on his apparent ability as a writer (and with the aid of an introduction from his headmaster) he got one in London with an advertising agency called Arks Publicity. Here he wrote copy for advertisements for 'bottled lime juice, radio valves, razor blades' (Rose's, Mullard's, and Wilkinson's respectively) and earned a salary of £1 a week. He was still solitary by habit and choice, lived modestly in a bedsittingroom in Westbourne Grove, and spent any spare money he had on theatre tickets, queueing whenever possible for the cheapest unreserved seats in the upper gallery.

This might have continued indefinitely, had it not been for a tiny mishap. One day Guinness was required to write and have set up an advertisement for Mullard Valves, intended for a prominent position on the front page of the *Daily Mail*. Though his mother wanted him to follow in his father's footsteps into a bank, he always maintained that he could never add two and two, and on this occasion he proceeded graphically to demonstrate as much. Dangerously late in the day, back came the block from the blockmaker, borne, to Guinness's surprise and alarm, by two men in a taxi. Inadvertently he had marked it to be made four feet by four feet, instead of four inches by four inches. The paper appeared with a significant gap, labelled 'This space reserved for Mullard Valves', and Guinness began seriously to wonder whether advertising was quite the ideal place for the exercise of whatever talents he might have. Not that he was fired on the spot: on the contrary, everyone was very kind and long-suffering, even if from that moment he was treated rather like the village idiot.

But it was evidently time to think of moving on. And his weekly visits to the Old Vic (usually walking home because he could not afford the bus fare) had really confirmed his feeling that above all he wanted to be an actor ('I just wanted to be someone else, to be in makeup, in disguise'). The question was, how to go about it. Among the other theatres he had visited – several times – was the New Theatre, where John Gielgud was having at that time a long and successful run in *Richard of Bordeaux*, playing Gordon Daviot's glamorous version of Richard II rather than Shakespeare's more unsparing vision of the character. Of the brilliant young actors just then establishing themselves in the London theatre, Gielgud was the one whom Guinness above all revered, so when he somehow got hold of Gielgud's phone number he just rang him up to ask for advice. Gielgud was very nice about it ('I would be bloody if anyone did that to me,' the mature Guinness reflected), and gave him instant practical advice that he should start by taking voice lessons from someone like Martita Hunt, who would in any case be glad of the money.

He took the advice, and invested in twelve lessons. Whether they did him any good he was never too sure; certainly they added Martita Hunt's opinion to that of others who had been all too ready to assert he would never make an actor. All the same, diffident and unprepossessing or not, he must have had some sort of inner confidence, or at least the strain of obstinacy which many who subsequently worked with him had reason to observe. For, far from being put off, he decided that the next step should be to try to get into RADA. Given his financial situation, it would have to be on one of their (very few) scholarships, and so, when the appointed time came, he paid his audition fee and turned up all prepared with extracts from Chekhov's *Three Sisters* and from *Henry V*, as well as an impersonation of George Arliss playing Disraeli. It was only to be told that there was no point in his auditioning at all, as there were no scholarships available for that year.

The first professional appearance on stage: as a junior counsel in Libel!

Crestfallen, he wandered away and by chance ran into a young woman whom he had known years before, when they were just a boy and a girl playing together on a beach. She had meanwhile become an actress, and hearing of his troubles told him to rush straight round to the private drama school then run by the distinguished actress Fay Compton, where they were at that moment holding scholarship auditions. With his material ready prepared he got the scholarship, which paid his tuition fees (he suspected it was the George Arliss imitation which did the trick). With the twenty-six shillings a week from his father's fund he could just about scrape by, living mainly on baked beans. Then, even though he won first prize – a leather-bound volume of Shakespeare – in a school competition judged by Gielgud (the first time he had met his idol face-to-face) and Jessie Matthews, fresh, presumably, from their triumph together in the film of *The Good Companions*, disaster struck. His allowance stopped abruptly. His presumed father, Andrew Geddes, had died in 1928, when Alec was 14, but may perhaps have set up a fund which would last until Alec was 20: Alec never knew the details. But whyever it happened, it meant that Guinness was in a quite desperate situation, reduced to living on apples, milk and an occasional jam sandwich made for him by the wife of a fellow-student, would-be actor Richard Hearne.

Clearly, he had to get a job. The previous year he had done a few days work as an extra on Victor Saville's melodramatic musical *Evensong*, with Evelyn Laye, and earned a guinea a day for it. But that was hardly something to make a career out of. In his first term at Fay Compton's he had managed to get a non-speaking role as a junior counsel in Edward Wooll's trial drama *Libel!*, one of a number of students who made up the numbers in the stage courtroom – and was paid twelve shillings a week for his pains. Now something more serious was required. Immediately after his triumph winning the prize in the end-of-year public performance (with, it is recorded, a speech of Mercutio, a major role in a mime-play by Compton Mackenzie about a homicidal Punch-and-Judy man, and singing – out of tune, no doubt – 'Waiting at the Gate for Katie') he was out, penniless, on the street.

Again he turned to Gielgud for advice. Gielgud was by this time appearing in *The Maitlands* at Wyndham's Theatre, and Guinness presented himself in his dressing room (the same star dressing room which he, by an odd coincidence, was to occupy thirty-four years later while playing in *Wise Child*). Gielgud again was a model of practicality. He told Guinness of an audition the next day and instructed him to go to it and report back the following evening. Guinness had no luck at the audition but reported back as required, and went through exactly the same routine for the three following days, each time with nothing good to report. Finally, when he came to the dressing room, he saw £20 laid out in crisp new notes on the table, and Gielgud said to him with brusque kindness 'You're not eating enough. You could use a good meal. Take that money until you can find a job.' The

1. *Aubrey Mather*
2. *Malcolm Keen*
3. *Frances Doble*
4. *Basil Dignam*
5. *Beckett Bould*
6. *Anthony Hollis*
7. *Leon M. Lion*
8. *Sir Nigel Playfair*
9. *Michael Barry*
10. *Joe Mitchenson*
11. *Alec Guinness*
12. *Mark Dignam*
13. *Twigge Molecey*
14. *John Stewart Bingley*

money must have seemed like a king's ransom, seeing that at that time Guinness's idea of real luxury was a full three-course meal at a Lyon's Corner House for 1/6d. But though he had only a few pence in his pockets he was too proud to accept, pretended that everything was much better than it was, and staggered out, dizzy with hunger, to walk back to his Bayswater attic.

He had not got very far – but at least past the glittering Mecca of Lyon's Coventry Street Corner House – when some strange impulse drove him to drop in at the Piccadilly Theatre and ask hopelessly at the box-office if there was any work going for actors. As it happened, the stage manager was there at the time, and struck by something in the young man's demeanour – or himself just desperate to fill a hole in the current production – got him to read and hired him on the spot as an understudy and bit-player for Noel Langley's play *Queer Cargo*, in which he appeared as a Chinese coolie in Act I, a French pirate in Act II, and an English sailor in Act III. While he was not exactly an overnight sensation, it was a start, and remarkably enough from then on, apart from the unavoidable gap of the war years, he was never out of work as an actor, except by his own choice.

The *Queer Cargo* experience also offered a couple of other significant pointers to Guinness's future. For the various acting and understudying jobs he was doing he was initially offered £2 a week. Desperate as he was for work, he quietly baulked at that – was not, he inquired, the minimum laid down by Equity £3? The stage manager warned him not to be 'bolshy' about such things if he wanted to get on in the business. So Guinness said no more, but the next day discreetly called Equity on the question. He got his £3, and ever afterwards supported Equity solidly in all its efforts to better the actor's lot, since it had once importantly done as much for him. The other pointer was more odd than anything else. Taking his responsibilities with all due seriousness (or perhaps more seriousness than was strictly due), he shaved his head for the coolie role and disguised the shining cranium with wigs or headgear for his other appearances in the play. The trouble was, as he ruefully observed afterwards, that the hair never really grew back. It was devastating for an aspiring actor of twenty-one to find that he was balding – even if, like Guinness, he never quite saw himself as a dashing romantic lead. But then, he reasoned, if the hair was going to go, it would go anyway, and settled his mind to the fact: on stage or screen he would wear whatever false hair the role seemed to require – it is, after all, merely an extension of costume and makeup – but in private life he would go, if that was what nature intended for him, bald-headed into the world.

His spell in *Queer Cargo* concluded, he was invited by his adviser and (increasingly) friend John Gielgud to join a company he was heading at the New Theatre for some eighteen months, from November 1934 to July 1936. It must have been a young actor's dream. He was being paid £7 a week, which was, if not lavish, at least a living wage. The role he was first given, Osric in Gielgud's *Hamlet*,

OPPOSITE: *as the Apothecary in* Romeo and Juliet, *with John Gielgud.*

was small, but he could make something of it, and the critics noticed. He then got to play roles of astonishing variety in André Obey's *Noah* (the famous production by Michel Saint-Denis), *Romeo and Juliet*, and *The Seagull*, in which he began as the Workman and graduated before the end of the run to Yakov.

Gielgud he found a hard but stimulating task-master. For a while he thought his great opportunity was over before it had begun, when during rehearsals for the *Hamlet* (which finally ran for 155 performances) Gielgud suddenly burst out 'I can't bear it. I can't bear it. Go away for ten days and learn to act, for God's sake.' He did as he was told, not sure whether he had been fired or not, and after a little while (less, certainly, than the ten days stipulated) went back and found that the problem had blown over. Gielgud's unpredictability and confident instinct for theatrical effect fascinated him and amazed him, and the personal influence exerted by his magnetic stage presence was something which, once Guinness had graduated to leading roles himself, he found very difficult to throw off. The other director of the season, Michel Saint-Denis, had considerably less effect on him: Saint-Denis's sense of theatrical stylisation, of finding the right image for the production, impressed him, but he found Saint-Denis's enthusiasm for the ideas of Stanislavsky unsympathetic when it came to getting performances out of individual actors, and the very opposite of his own instincts in the matter. Even at this early stage in his career, Guinness had recognised that for him the way to the heart of a character was through the externals: get the look, the facial expression, the tone of voice, the walk right, and the inner man would surely take care of himself.

But perhaps Guinness's most important encounter of all during this period was with another member of the company. In *Noah* he played the Wolf, and the Tiger was played by a very quiet young redhead called Merula Salaman. These two natural loners hit it off very well together but, characteristically for both of them, did not rush precipitately into anything: they had known each other for three years before they finally got married in 1938 and went off for their honeymoon to a house belonging to Tyrone Guthrie in western Ireland, far from 'civilisation' but close to the Monaghan Lakes, where Guinness could pursue his enjoyed (but, he asserted, spectacularly unsuccessful) hobby of fishing. It would be hard to overestimate the importance to Guinness, with his own shaky family background, of a loving, secure marriage to a like-minded being with a devotion to privacy equalling if not excelling his own. Here, at least, his life very definitely has no history: Merula cut down her acting career without a pang to become Mrs Alec Guinness, giving it up completely when he returned from his war service, and remained happily his sheet anchor for more than sixty years.

STAGE STAR

When the memorable Gielgud season came to an end in July 1936, Guinness went with scarcely a pause into the next season at the Old Vic, starting in September. He had by this time established himself as a useful and versatile young character actor, with a particular gift for portraying those loons and courtiers who people the corners of Shakespeare's plays and, reasonably frequently, move close enough to the centre to be recognised and relished. That description fits exactly five out of the six roles he was to play at the Old Vic, while the sixth was a doddering ancient in a play of the Shakespearean era, *The Witch of Edmonton*. That was directed by Michel Saint-Denis, but all the others were directed by the next extraordinary theatrical force Guinness was to encounter, Tyrone Guthrie.

Guthrie, at thirty-six, was director of the Old Vic Company for his second season (the first was 1933–34, when Guinness was first a regular member of the audience), and was regarded as a young Turk, if not the young Turk, of the British theatre. Very much a director's director, he impressed his own idiosyncratic personality firmly on whatever he touched, and as against the strict physical discipline of a Gielgud production and the deep mental discipline of a Saint-Denis production, he believed in keeping his actors on a loose rein, as free to improvise as he was himself. The result was generally something at one extreme or another: he dealt in triumphs or disasters, with nothing much in between; his productions were either definitive or perverse to a degree which left critics and public gasping. Clearly he responded at once to Guinness's extreme peculiarity, a quality which could be used, and to his already evident self-discipline, which meant that the peculiarity would always be kept firmly within professional bounds. Guinness, for his part, found the relative freedom of a Guthrie production stimulating and rapidly became a close personal friend of his mercurial director.

During the season September 1936–April 1937 he played assorted courtiers and loons under Guthrie's direction in *Love's Labour's Lost*, *As You Like It*, *Hamlet* (Osric again, to Olivier's Hamlet), *Henry V* and *Twelfth Night*. Few of the roles were exactly designed to launch a star – only a very knowledgeable Shakespearean could summon up an instant image of Boyet in *Love's Labour's Lost*, or of Exeter in *Henry V* – but one, Aguecheek in *Twelfth Night*, was something to shine in, and Guinness shone. With a makeup which emphasised an already existent resemblance to Stan Laurel (remarked on independently by at least three first-night critics), Guinness played the foolish knight as someone perpetually a little out of step with life, still reacting to the line or the happening before last while everyone else in the world sweeps inexorably on. It was wonderfully funny, and also oddly touching: not for the last time, Guinness was placed in the long line of classic clowns, and if any single role defined him and his talents for audiences in the thirties, it was undoubtedly this. Of course it was not his largest or most important role – after all, within a year or so he was

ABOVE: as Boyet in Tyrone Guthrie's production of Love's Labour's Lost.

RIGHT: as Osric in Hamlet *at the Old Vic (1937) with Laurence Olivier and Robert Newton.*

LEFT: *as Exeter in* Henry V *with Laurence Olivier and Harcourt Williams.*

OPPOSITE: *as Sir Andrew Aguecheek in* Twelfth Night, *with Laurence Olivier as Sir Toby Belch.*

BELOW: *the programme of the 1937 Old Vic Shakespeare Birthday Festival.*

MR. SNAKE AND LADY SNEERWELL

Opposite, top: as Lorenzo in The Merchant of Venice, *and below: as Aumerle in* Richard II *with John Gielgud.*

Below: Tom Titt's caricature of Guinness and Dorothy Green in The School for Scandal *and right, as Snake with Gielgud and Dorothy Green.*

playing his own Hamlet – but it was the one which stuck most firmly in the minds of theatregoers, and so continued to influence the way people saw him even after the war.

Before his next season at the Old Vic and his Hamlet, Guinness took his Osric to Elsinore, and played another season with Gielgud's company, this time at the Queen's Theatre. In this he was directed by all three of his mentors: Gielgud in *Richard II* and *The Merchant of Venice*, Guthrie in *The School for Scandal*, and Saint-Denis in *The Three Sisters*. Though the critics had good words for him as the malicious Snake in *The School of Scandal*, he would have seemed to be standing still in his career but for the astonishing success of his Lorenzo in *The Merchant of Venice*. It is not a role anyone can make very much of – or so one would have thought. But it does contain in the last act some of Shakespeare's most exquisite poetry, introducing at last into this rather nasty tale of unpleasant people a touch of true romantic passion. That is not, of course, a register which, at this stage or later, is associated particularly with Guinness, and so Kenneth Tynan was probably not too far from the mark when he linked Guinness's enraptured performance with the external fact of his marriage in that very summer.

For the moment, however, there were other considerations beside

C GUINNESS, DOROTHY GREEN

the merely romantic view. It was time for Guinness to take his first leading role, even if in the relative obscurity of the outer suburbs, in Richmond. (It should be noted at this point that all his stage career, from the beginning, had been in London: a record virtually unique in a country where – and at a time when – practically every great career was firmly founded on the crammed routine of a provincial repertory or a national tour.) The play was Shaw's *The Doctor's Dilemma*, and the role was that of Louis Dubedat, the impossible, self-centred, shifty and unreliable artist for whom allowances must be made (according to Shavian canons at least) because he is a genius. One important inducement to Guinness to take the role was that the wife, Jennifer Dubedat, was to be played by the American actress Carol Goodner, who had just starred in the production of *The Three Sisters* where he had played Fedotik. But even more important, the role of Louis fitted him like a glove, offering a brilliant showcase for many of his most distinctive talents. It cannot have been entirely by chance that one of his best roles, when he had reached a position of maturity and power to choose, was a virtual re-run of the role in a different register, Gulley Jimpson in *The Horse's Mouth* (1958), and that not only did he play the part to perfection, but he wrote the screenplay as well.

After this interlude slightly away from the centre of things, that autumn Guinness was back with the Old Vic, facing his biggest challenge to date: his first Hamlet in what was bound to be a controversial modern-dress production by Tyrone Guthrie. In the first production

ABOVE: the first leading role, advertised in the local paper.

BELOW: as Arthur Glover in Trelawny of the 'Wells', *with Sophie Stewart and O.B. Clarence.*

of the season, Pinero's *Trelawny of the 'Wells'*, he played a fairly minor role, as Arthur Cower, the romantic hero from whom all the best scenes are stolen by the rag, tag and bobtail of the early Victorian theatrical profession who surround him. Then, in October, came *Hamlet*. It is hard to know how that should be categorised. It was certainly not one of Guthrie's (and therefore by extension Guinness's) disastrous follies. The shock of modern dress was in general well-received, even the 'Peter Grimes' attire of fisherman's sweater and gumboots in which Guinness was required to tackle the graveyard scene. Guinness himself received polite, and in some quarters enthusiastic notices, and at least no one doubted that his very played-down Hamlet was perfectly in key with the tone of the whole production. But wasn't it, several critics rather tentatively asked, a bit *too* played-down? It was a Hamlet which not so much failed to soar as deliberately refused to: the loner, so lost in his own private morass of moral indecision that he could hardly connect with any one else on stage and all too frequently seemed to gabble or mumble his lines, almost without expression. It was not possible to doubt that this was

ABOVE AND RIGHT: the modern-dress Hamlet *with Hermione Hannan (Ophelia) and Malcolm Keen (The Ghost).*

ABOVE: Angus McBean's portrait study of Guinness as Hamlet.

a deliberate strategy on Guinness's part, and the reading could there-fore fairly be described as 'controversial', the term being used for once in its correct sense rather than as a euphemism for 'universally damned'. James Agate was discriminating but not unsympathetic: he called Guinness's performance 'non-acting', but felt that it came, 'in the end, to have a value of its own.' What no one could guess at the time, of course, that here was the key to Guinness's whole future career: the resolutely inward, anti-rhetorical style which he essayed first on a large scale in *Hamlet*, and did not then have enough authority to project as a positive value, was to become in later years the hall-mark of his acting, what made his performances so mysteriously compelling, what made him, in a word, unique.

Having emerged with honour from his first major role in a major London theatre, he settled down to consolidation. His last new role at the Old Vic that season was Bob Acres in *The Rivals*, and it comes

RIGHT: as Bob Acres in The Rivals.

BELOW: George Whitelaw's cartoon of Guinness and Anthony Quayle in The Rivals.

as no surprise that while most actors played him as a galumphing idiot, Guinness, without losing the humour, managed to invest his character with a very characteristic sort of wayward discombobula-tion: yet another character who could not, like Hamlet or Aguecheek, quite connect satisfactorily with the world around him. After an extended tour with the Old Vic in Europe and the Middle East, play-ing all the same roles as well as starring in *Libel!*, where not so long before he had been the most humble supernumerary, he returned to the Old Vic Theatre for a single role, that of the explorer Ransom in

the W.H. Auden/Christopher Isherwood play *The Ascent of* F6. He was not yet creating a role, but the critics all felt that he was much more at home in this depiction of another mysterious genius than the actor who had played it on its first appearance three years before. Clearly, Guinness was just the kind of person of whom one could believe remarkable things: an oddball and a misfit, maybe, but also perhaps the sort of genius who could transform the world. One intriguing point does arise in relation to *The Ascent of F6*, and it is probably very relevant to our understanding of Guinness's character. At the time he told various interviewers that he was drawn to the play and the role because the character of Ransom was evidently (and admittedly) suggested to some extent by T.E. Lawrence, and Lawrence was one of his heroes. Now Lawrence was, whichever way you look at him, one of those tortured, introvert geniuses that Guinness always seemed to identify very readily with: the man of

ABOVE: The Ascent of F6, *with Frederick Peisley, Arthur Macrae, Laurier Lister and Ernest Hare.*

action who is also a thinker. Obviously this combination must represent the secret aspiration of an actor who is also a thinker but finds that thinking too much can often be an impediment to action. Typically, when Guinness actually came to play Lawrence on stage more than twenty years later, in *Ross*, his expressed opinion of the man was very different.

And right away, any secret desires he might have to cut a romantic figure were thoroughly dashed, where it must have hurt most: in his professional life. For he went on to make, by general consent, one of his few major professional errors. It was probably just as well it happened in the decent obscurity of Perth. Despite his success with Lorenzo, Romeo was not and never would be his role: neither the poetic romantic like Gielgud, nor the dashing extrovert like Olivier, he found that here was a role he could not possibly play with the tortured inwardness he had brought to Hamlet. It was just outside his range, and that was that. And so, he perhaps ruefully recognised,

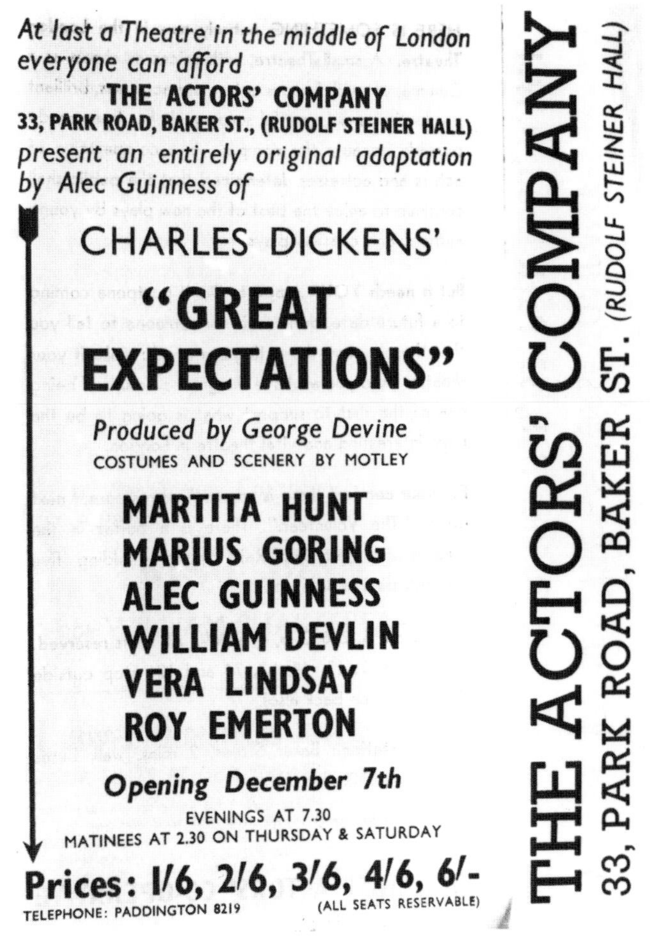

RIGHT: poster for the Actors' Company production of Guinness's Great Expectations.

At last a Theatre in the middle of London everyone can afford

THE ACTORS' COMPANY

33, PARK ROAD, BAKER ST., (RUDOLF STEINER HALL)

present an entirely original adaptation by Alec Guinness of

CHARLES DICKENS'

"GREAT EXPECTATIONS"

Produced by George Devine

COSTUMES AND SCENERY BY MOTLEY

MARTITA HUNT
MARIUS GORING
ALEC GUINNESS
WILLIAM DEVLIN
VERA LINDSAY
ROY EMERTON

Opening December 7th

EVENINGS AT 7.30
MATINEES AT 2.30 ON THURSDAY & SATURDAY

Prices: 1/6, 2/6, 3/6, 4/6, 6/-

TELEPHONE: PADDINGTON 8219   (ALL SEATS RESERVABLE)

THE ACTORS' COMPANY (RUDOLF STEINER HALL)
33, PARK ROAD, BAKER ST.

were General Wolfe and Captain Cook and the other successful leaders of men he distantly admired: on stage he had to be content with
being wise, or a fool, or if possible both. His great gift was for finding the extraordinary hidden within the ordinary, the poetry locked in
the prose of life.

The demonstration of his unsuitability as Romeo was followed
immediately by a triumph in what we would normally have thought
of as a thoroughly unsuitable role – combined with a very decent success in another role entirely. Guinness had always been good at
English while at school, and nurtured desires – not so unusual in an
actor if we think of Michael Redgrave, Alec McCowen, Dirk Bogarde
– to be a writer. Little knowing that soon enough writing would for
several years be his only practical creative outlet, he now boldly
appeared before the public as a playwright. On a modest enough
scale, to be sure: an adaptation of a Dickens' novel staged by a new,
not very commercial management, The Actors' Company (which con-
sisted primarily of Guinness, Marius Goring and the director George
Devine), off the usual theatrical track at the Rudolph Steiner Hall,
was not, perhaps risking too much. On the other hand it was no
doubt as far as he was able to venture at this stage in his career, and
the sensitivity and intelligence with which *Great Expectations* was
adapted certainly received favourable attention. His triumph, though,
was in the role he himself chose to play, Herbert Pocket. The quintessential best friend, always on the sidelines, it would have been a
surprising choice for any actor-playwright except Guinness, and even
with Guinness it was odd, because Pocket is such an open, sociable,
communicative creature, the absolute opposite of Guinness's usual
tortured solitary or droll misfit. It was a performance which so
charmed people that they remembered. And among those who
remembered, so it would seem, was a certain young film editor called
David Lean…

STOP AND START

At this time, December 1939, the war in Europe had begun, but had settled down, after a few initial flurries of near-panic, into its 'phony' stage: the expected hail of bombs failed for the moment to descend, and everything at home in Britain seemed tranced in a state of suspension. Guinness continued quietly to progress along his chosen route, achieving his first major West End role in a new play with Clemence Dane's *Cousin Muriel* at the Globe. It was not a very thrilling experience, nor did it last very long, even though it gave him an opportunity to act opposite Edith Evans and seemed, in its lighthearted look at kleptomania, to be pitched right for a public that for the moment wanted diversion rather than something really demanding. In the summer Guinness was back at the Old Vic, playing Ferdinand to Gielgud's Prospero in *The Tempest*, and then in the autumn he had his first real experience of English provincial theatre (it was to be virtually his last), touring in Robert Ardrey's *Thunder Rock* in the role Michael Redgrave had created on the London stage. Redgrave was striking as the lighthouse keeper running away from himself who is pushed back into life by hearing the story of the ghosts who surround him in his solitude. But equally the role was perfect for Guinness, exploiting all his distinctive qualities outside the realm of humour to maximum effect.

PREVIOUS PAGE: making up as de Guiche in Cyrano de Bergerac.

GLOBE
THEATRE

6⁻

EDITH EVANS
IN
COUSIN MURIEL
BY
CLEMENCE DANE

LEFT: with Edith Evans, AND OPPOSITE, with Peggy Ashcroft in Cousin Muriel.

LEFT: as Ferdinand in The Tempest, *with John Gielgud and Jessica Tandy*

But already the phony war was giving place to a real war, and the drama of outside events taking over from drama behind the footlights. At the beginning of 1941 Guinness went into the Navy as an ordinary seaman. It was the beginning, as he put it, of 'a very, very small part, but a long, long run'. He was to have, as they said at the time, a 'good war': after about six months in the ranks he was commissioned, and made commander of a small coastal vessel – crew about twenty – for use mainly in the Mediterranean. Here he played his small part primarily by ferrying supplies to the Yugoslav partisans – by his own account a very humdrum occupation, though here one suspects a certain amount of decent stiff-upper-lippery comes into play. Meanwhile, on the home front, his only child, Matthew, was born in 1941, a source of great pride and joy to such a private, family man.

The quiet routine of a mere war was broken only once by a call back to the world he had temporarily forsaken. Terence Rattigan's patriotic drama of life in the RAF at war, *Flare Path*, written during the intervals of his war service in Africa, had scored an enormous sentimental success in London when staged in August 1942; it ended by running nearly two years. Obviously, as well as holding out a decided possibility of repeating its commercial success in America, such a play could do invaluable service from a propaganda point of view. At the time Guinness happened to be in America on not-very-active service, waiting for his ship to be refitted in Boston, so he seemed a natural to play the hero, a superficially bluff, insensitive

OPPOSITE: in Flare Path, *with Nancy Kelly.*

bomber pilot who unconsciously manages to keep his wife from leaving him by revealing to her his own inner vulnerability. Guinness always maintained he never knew why he was chosen – 'only available actor with an English accent', he unconvincingly suggested. But chosen he was, and temporarily released from his war service for this other, more specialised kind of war work. It was his first appearance on the New York stage, and in less outwardly disturbing circumstances it would have been an exciting opportunity for any young actor – especially in a role he should be able to play well, Herbert Pocket on the outside and the hero of *Thunder Rock* underneath. But unfortunately it was not to be. Despite a carefully cast and rehearsed production, directed by Margaret Webster, the play was adjudged too gentlemanly and restrained for American tastes, and Rattigan's dialogue too specifically English for ready comprehension. It opened the day before Christmas Eve, 1942, at the Henry Miller Theatre, and closed after precisely two weeks. This was long enough, at least, for Twentieth Century-Fox to offer Guinness a screen-test in Hollywood, seeing him as possibly a new Robert Donat figure. It was tempting, certainly, especially in the light of lines he was saying on stage every night about the sheer terror of going into action. But on the other hand Guinness did not feel for one moment that he had any alternative to returning when his special assignment was over.

So back to his ship, and whenever possible his writing, went Guinness. He took comfort in writing home as much as time and the military censors allowed – to his wife primarily, but also to friends like Sir Sydney Cockerell, stalwart survivor from the era of William Morris and the Arts and Crafts movement. He also managed to do some more formal writing, and his efforts were rewarded by appearance in that great wartime standby *Penguin New Writing*, an anthology of the best new writing then coming out at home and abroad in a paperback format suitable to be stuffed into a soldier's kitbag or even a civilian gasmask case. Probably the most widely read piece of writing Guinness produced at this time was somewhere between the informality of a letter and the more careful shaping of a story or an essay: a long letter edited for publication in the *Daily Telegraph* of 20 August 1943 under the title 'I Took My Landing Craft to the Sicily Beaches'.

This describes, in admirably direct, human terms, the Allied landing in Sicily on 9 July 1943 – the lapse of time was enforced by the stringent requirements of the censor. According to the version of the story which has become legend, Guinness was in fact the first man ashore, having mistaken or failed to receive a signal and gone in an hour early. In his contemporary account it all sounds much more orderly than that – either from tact on his part, or because he was simply recording a happening which others would later turn into an event. However, it does seem to be true that his landing-craft actually led the attack, following the commandos in, because what

was supposed to be the leader had got lost during the night, and he was number two. This detail certainly gives colour to the other half of the received legend, which is that when his Admiral finally turned up Guinness smartly reproved him with the observation that lateness of that sort would *never* be tolerated in the theatre. Perhaps the most characteristic and telling observation in Guinness's piece comes in the tail, however, when he reflects, with determined evenness of tone:

'Many other ships had as uneventful a time as I did, but there were yet others – and maybe they did not. But on the whole it was as if the Italians wanted us to come, and only made a little resistance to avoid being clouted over the head by their German brothers.

'How dull, how dull all this is. And yet, presumably, it's a good sized page in the history books already.'

In later life, Lieutenant Guinness suggested in the best traditional manner that he was cheerily vague and incompetent but somehow muddled through. He insisted that in convoy he always had great difficulty keeping his ship in line, until he received a cryptic communication from the flagship: 'Hebrews 13:8'. Which, duly interpreted with the aid of the ship's Bible, meant 'Jesus Christ, the same yesterday, and today, and forever.' He also recalled that after the Sicily landing his supply ship was destroyed in a 120-mile-an-hour gale which blew it right across the Adriatic on to the rocks of Termoli. Luckily his whole crew managed to get ashore safely, and though he subsequently felt convinced the Admiralty longed to blame the loss on him, since another dozen ships had been wrecked in the same storm it did not look too much like his personal, unique incompetence, and before long they put him in command of another vessel.

Before he got back to the supplying of partisans, however, he stayed close to the armies invading Italy, and was involved also in the Anzio beachhead. And there he very probably encountered someone, though neither could be aware of it at the time, that he was subsequently going to know well and star with. Up at Pozzuoli, just north of Naples, there was a small stall on the quayside where servicemen could get coffee and imitation brandy, while the local children ran round begging for chocolate, chewing-gum or anything else they had to give. Twenty years later Guinness was telling this to Sophia Loren, with whom he was appearing in *The Fall of the Roman Empire*, and she pointed out that she knew all about it, as she had been one of those same children round the coffee-seller.

As the war in Europe drew finally to its close, Guinness was still with supply-boats, now around the coast of Greece. Whence came the 'Epic of the Yellow Duck'. It can probably best be told in Guinness's own words, relayed to *The Times* by Sir Sydney Cockerell as from 'a well-known actor in the R.N.V.R., who has changed the part of Hamlet for that of the commander of an unnamed vessel, perhaps HMS Pinafore.'

OPPOSITE: Guinness, RN, as caricatured by Sherriffs at the time of Barnacle Bill *(1957).*

41

Somewhere in the Mediterranean

My ship's company are busy making toys for Greek children.
I've even made a large woollen ball myself which caused a
great deal of amusement among my more masculine friends.
We happen to know a wretchedly poor Greek convent, where
eighty small children, all orphans, are cared for. The very best
that can be done for them is done – but it amounts to
practically nothing – they are more than half-starved. Many of
the babies are red raw – because they have to be washed in
sea water, fresh water being so precious that it can only be
spared for drinking. None of them has ever known a sweet or
seen any sort of toy. The proud possession of the children was
a small ring of steel which could be rolled along the floor –
not even a tin to beat with a stick – for every tin is required as
a cooking utensil, and all sticks are fuel.
    A naval officer I know happened to have a wooden yellow
duck on wheels on board – it was an intended Christmas
present for a niece in England. He presented it to the
convent, it caused stupefaction! It was received with wide-
eyed silence and gaping mouths – and then solemnly led by a
daring four-year-old out into the street. In absolute silence all
the children followed it, and soon a regular procession was
started, with old men and women, soldiers, priests, everyone –
and they all followed the yellow duck through the main street
of the town. Someone found a Union Jack and hoisted it on a
pole. A tatttered, dirty drummer appeared from somewhere,
and a fiddler with a squeaky fiddle. They played, almost
unrecognizably, 'God Save the King'. And the yellow duck, a
hideosity, was finally led, like the Trojan horse, back into the
convent – and so we make toys for them now and hope to get
them to the kids before Christmas.

Finally it was time for actors in the services, like everyone else, to go
home. The release was, for Guinness as for many others, long in coming. After all, he had been an actor of note before the war, but not,
like Olivier or Richardson or Gielgud, exactly part of our national
heritage. The British Theatre (with defiant capitals) could hardly continue without them, but without Guinness it could, as far as anyone
knew, manage very well. It would be nice to have him back, of course,
but nobody was in any great rush. Not even, perhaps, Guinness himself. Always inclined to self-doubt, he certainly had the gravest doubts
about what kind of talent he had possessed, and whether he still had
it. A further brief release from duty to appear in a charity pageant
hardly constituted the new trial of his own abilities he needed to reas-
sure himself, and then he had always had this ambition to be a writer.

Should he, perhaps, give up acting altogether, assuming that he had, during the five years he had been away from his craft, grown into a different person with different priorities? Deep down he did not believe that: again it was a need for reassurance, and he reacted sharply enough when a wise friend told him firmly that he must choose between writing and acting: 'This was very flattering to my prose, but inside I was outraged – he was casting aspersions on my acting.'

Without a doubt, some hard thinking had to be done. But at least Guinness was finally allowed to go home – to the comfortable house in a rundown London square which he had hardly seen, to the son now pushing five whom he had to get really to know for the first time, and to Merula. There he could retire and contemplate. And, whatever he decided, he could lay his plans carefully...

When he bade the West End stage a temporary farewell which might not, for all he or anyone else knew, be so temporary, Alec Guinness was twenty-six and already a star: one who had taken the necessary hurdle of *Hamlet* at a gallop, and won the plaudits of the London drama critics as the most promising young – very young – addition to the long roll of classical actors in the English theatre. When he returned, he was – what? Thirty-two, for one thing. Still young, of course, but what would the loss of those vital formative years mean – years, after all, which should normally have taken him from promise to fulfilment? Clearly he could not just take up again where he had left off: the theatre was not the same, the world was not the same, and, most importantly of all, he was not the same. If audiences remembered him at all (and it was a big if) they probably remembered someone different, and now he had to begin again to conquer them.

But at least he was still there – unlike, for instance, Stephen Haggard, an equally promising talent who had blazed through the theatre, specializing in sensitive adolescents and neurotic young men, before disappearing into the Intelligence Corps and to death in action in the Middle East. Haggard had also written a novel, a play and a quantity of poetry, and was remembered more than others of his generation only because his writing talents had left material for two more posthumously published books, *I'll Go to Bed at Noon* and an exchange of letters on comedy with Athiene Seyler. Guinness had, despite the inevitable setback of the war years, much to be thankful for. But it can hardly have been without trepidation that he prepared to step once more into the limelight. He had, it is true, a small taste of a London audience again in 1945, but it was a very small taste, and a very special audience, when he played Nelson in the Navy's patriotic pageant *Heart of Oak* at the Albert Hall. The real test would come when he had to assume a leading role in a major production before an audience not swayed by any purpose more (or less) serious than to see good theatre well acted and get entertainment value for their money.

In the event, characteristically, Guinness chose to take on more than one challenge simultaneously: not only did he play Mitya in *The Brothers Karamazov*, which anyway seems like jumping in at the deep end, but he was himself responsible for the stage adaptation of Dostoevsky's complex and sprawling novel. It was put on at the Lyric, Hammersmith, that curiously ambiguous theatre which, though geographically far from the West End, has always seemed spiritually to belong there rather than in its own rather drab western suburb. Peter Brook directed; then himself just twenty-one, and already the most talked-about young director in the British theatre, he was an astute choice and garnered much of the critical attention the show received with a production of unremitting fury and intensity. After the production itself, Frederick Valk stole the show (or at least the reviews) with his oversize portrayal of that oversize character old Karamazov, the father of the varied and ill-fated brothers.

And there, not exactly on the sidelines but not really centre-stage either, was Guinness. In his own adaptation of *Great Expectations* he had chosen to play Herbert Pocket, a frankly marginal character. Mitya is certainly not marginal; in any reasonably accurate rendering of *The Brothers Karamazov* – and Guinness's adaptation was by general consent at least that – each of the brothers gets his moments of full audience attention. But his haunted personality requires of the actor intensity rather than variety, an inward smouldering rather than the outpouring of the rest. Guinness's Mitya, wrapped up in himself and greeting any attempt to penetrate with savage scorn, was a constantly disconcerting presence on stage, a man whose mental and spiritual isolation mark him out instantly in any company, however he may apparently throw himself into social activity. Again, in the new conditions of the postwar theatre, Guinness was playing a loner and an obsessive. And even for those who had not seen his Hamlet, the impact was unforgettable: he might not be the first thing you thought of, seeing *Karamazov*, but he would certainly be the lasting memory.

So, he was back. And in some respects it was almost as though he had never been away. It still needed a real West End success to clinch it, though, and that was not long in coming. *Karamazov* had been in June; the next month he opened, again under the direction of Peter Brook, in Sartre's *Huis Clos*, called in English translation *Vicious Circle*, at the Arts Theatre. After the long culture-gap of the war, Britain was about to discover what had been going on in the French theatre and cinema since the last direct contacts in the thirties. Names like Sartre, Anouilh and Camus were beginning to appear in excited reports of what had been and was happening on the other side of the Channel, and *Huis Clos* attracted special attention as one of the first opportunities London playgoers had been offered to judge for themselves.

For his role of Garcin, the man trapped in Sartre's view of hell, a nondescript room somewhere out of time when the misdeeds of a life are endlessly mulled over and re-enacted, and from which there is no

As Mitya in his own adaptation of The Brothers Karamazov, *with Pierre Lefevre (ABOVE) and Elizabeth Sellars (OPPOSITE).*

escape because no possibility of free choice, Guinness was required to age, leave off the wild wig he had worn as Mitya to reveal his own receding hairline, and embrace a premature middle age. His character is a man whose main aim in life – also in life-in-death, for all eternity – is to justify himself and prove he is not a coward in the eyes of the one woman who will never accept it. She sadistically but hopelessly desires the third member of the triangle, whose own desires are irrevocably fixed on the man, who finds her repellent and, worse, irrelevant. In 1946 this was pretty controversial stuff; the lesbian angle in particular ensured that the play could not hope for the Lord Chamberlain's seal of approval, and had to be done at a theatre club instead, where theatre censorship did not apply. But the Arts was the most distinguished of such clubs, the Mecca of those who wanted to sample all that was newest and most intelligent in current theatre. Later on it would provide a decent jumping-off point for Beckett, Ionesco and Pinter, and even in 1946 a production lost nothing (except maybe the possibility of a mass audience) by opening there.

Huis Clos duly created its sensation. A smallish, intellectual sensation, to be sure, but it meant that Guinness suddenly became again a name to conjure with, in Britain and the USA. Understandably, because his Garcin was one of the first of his magisterial studies of alienation: a character locked up in himself even before he is locked up with anyone else, somebody who has a secret life of his own, indicated only by little secret signs – a twitch at the corner of the mouth, a momentary inattention or hyperattention in the eyes – which he will

LEFT: in Vicious Circle (Huis Clos) *with Bette Ann Davis and Beatrix Lehmann, and above, as seen by* Punch.

fight to a standstill rather than expose to the world about him. Garcin's trouble with his own conscience, his own self-knowledge, is eventually exposed completely, but the battle to reach that point is something Guinness more than any actor of his generation was equipped to give full value, and the restrained, banked-up intensity of his performance at once made – or remade – him a star.

If he was tempted by this prospect, and especially by alluring offers from America, Guinness gave no sign of it. (Of course, he wouldn't.) Instead he took the traditional, respectable way of self-denial for the British actor: he joined the Old Vic company for a season. There, it is true, he was to be groomed for stardom of a rather different, but maybe surer and more solid kind, and he must have known it. He was, in principle, but a humble player in a company of many such, playing nice little roles which would be, or at any rate could be, noticed. He had specifically asked for it to be that way, requesting that he be given 'a total variety of parts for these two seasons, because I have no idea where my talent lies, or if it exists any more.' But the giants of the last few seasons, Olivier and Richardson, had gone or were about to go, and a new giant was desperately needed. Guinness, marked out by those in the know even before the war, seemed the obvious choice, and as well as the good supporting roles he was to have one chance to spread his wings, as Shakespeare's Richard II, directed by Ralph Richardson.

All was not plain sailing, however. No doubt it scarcely could be: Richard II was a character upon whom another actor, Gielgud, had definitively left his mark, and it is doubtful whether Guinness, even with his new status in the loftier sections of the West End theatre, was yet sufficiently distinct from Gielgud in his stage personality or carried enough authority of his own to revolutionise received ideas on the subject of Richard or even, in a less spectacular fashion, impose himself on the role. In addition, this was to be Richardson's first attempt at direction – a dangerous manoeuvre for what was meant, discreetly, to be a decisive stage in the company's development. As it happened, the fateful moment was put off by *force majeur*: it was one of the coldest winters on record, and as power cut followed power cut and backstage at the Old Vic the water froze in its pipes, the necessary rehearsals became quite out of the question. Meanwhile, Guinness continued to warm up (if that is the *mot juste*) with the smaller roles which were to precede the starring vehicle.

The first was the Fool in *Lear*, to Laurence Olivier's King – a sad, battered, loyal but slyly malicious figure, right in the centre of what was then assumed to be Guinness's range. Eric Birling in *An Inspector Calls*, J.B. Priestley's tricky postwar successor to his 'time plays', was not exactly the role that would give any actor much trouble: an unthinking young wastrel who proves not really so black-hearted after all, he filled out a strong cast in a so-so piece where, with hindsight, we would say now he was designed by nature to play the mysterious inspector, a character who is hardly there at all. The other

BELOW: Roger Furse's costume design for Guinness as the Fool in King Lear.

The Fool

47

LEFT AND ABOVE: *as the Fool to Laurence Olivier's King Lear.*

roles of the season were De Guiche, Cyrano's chilly and elegant rival in *Cyrano de Bergerac*, with Richardson as Cyrano, and Abel Drugger in Ben Jonson's *The Alchemist*. For this latter role he sported a tousled seventeenth-century crewcut, and made more of what is really a subsidiary role – an innocent tobacconist in thrall to Face, the alchemist's man (Richardson) – than any actor had done since Garrick. Kenneth Tynan singled him out: 'Mr Guinness manages to get to the heart of all good, hopeful young men who can enjoy without envy the company of wits'; and, more pointedly, recognised Guinness's peculiar ability to convey solitude, something he later defined as a gift for making each individual member of the audience feel like an eavesdropper, the only one privileged to observe.

So ended Guinness's first season at the Old Vic, with Richard still unassayed. But meanwhile he had already taken his first step along another road, one which was to prove perhaps more important in the

ABOVE: as Eric Birling in An Inspector Calls, *with Julian Mitchell, Ralph Richardson and Harry Andrews.*

RIGHT: as De Guiche to Ralph Richardson's Cyrano de Bergerac.

LEFT: as Abel Drugger in The Alchemist.

light of the future. During the summer he had made his first real appearance on film – discounting, that is, his early extra-work – by playing again the role of Herbert Pocket in David Lean's film of *Great Expectations*, and in December 1946 the film was released, to universal acclaim. Richard Winnington, for example, in the *News Chronicle*, summed it up as 'a lavish, unostentatious film, romantic, exciting and English to the core,' and listed Guinness (misspelt) among the 'nearly perfect' cast who managed 'never to lapse into Coloured Christmas Supplement portraits'. Other critics thought much the same; it could not be said that Guinness was specially singled out, but he was clearly credited as an admirable part of an immaculate whole.

Of course, anyone who cared to look closer at his Herbert Pocket might note that Tynan's description of his Abel Drugger could apply equally well here: Herbert is that perennial sidekick character, the hero's best friend who supports, comforts, possibly worships but never gets the girl, and does a lot of necessary running about to free the hero for the real drama. It is the kind of role generally described as 'thankless', and so it is, yet it needs someone very special to prevent

OPPOSITE: as Herbert Pocket in the film of Great Expectations *with Finlay Currie.*

106(II).

it from being merely part of the structure. And sometimes, as in the case of Abel Drugger, it gets a Garrick (or a Guinness) to make the most of it. It is odd, and interesting, that Guinness should have deliberately chosen to play Herbert in his own stage adaptation of Dickens' novel; presumably the idea of his playing the character again in the film came from someone's long memory, and the realisation that, with his unlined face and youthful manner, he could still play a very young man convincingly.

Possibly the memory was David Lean's. But whether at that point it was or not, from then on the teaming was to be highly advantageous for both of them. Guinness in fact was to prove through the years to be one of Lean's favourite actors, and each one of the six Lean films in which he appeared marked in some way a significant stage in his career: from his first screen appearance (always excepting the extra work on *Evensong*) through to his first principal role – Fagin in *Oliver Twist* is indeed arguably the starring role, next to that of Oliver himself – his first Oscar, for *Bridge on the River Kwai*, his first major character role in a super-production (Feisal in *Lawrence of Arabia*), a form of appearance which was to assume considerable importance in the pattern of Guinness's professional life; in *Doctor Zhivago*, a not-too-rewarding role which marked a rupture with Lean and a certain disenchantment with films on Guinness's part, and finally the reunion of the two grand old men in Lean's long-meditated version of E.M. Forster's *A Passage to India*. Oddly enough, there does not seem to have been much personal warmth between the two men: both seem to be regarded by those around them as men of mystery, very private persons, and criticism of Lean's films has often resolved itself, like criticism of Guinness's acting, into a search for the defining personality behind the immaculately impersonal, endistancing surface. Each was vocal in praise of the other's technical efficiency and immaculate craftsmanship, and their creative encounters seem usually to have brought out the best in both. But one wonders whether it was not an element of challenge in the situation, with each trying somehow to penetrate the other's defences, to know without being really known, which produced such extraordinary results.

Meanwhile, however, this was all very much in the future. Guinness had yet to establish himself securely as a leading player in either the theatre or the cinema, and there was a lot of lost ground to make up from the war years. The first big test could, in this context, have been more happily chosen.

A DOUBLE LIFE

Held over from the bitter winter, *Richard II* finally reached the stage of the Old Vic company, still in its temporary home at the New Theatre while the Old Vic theatre itself was being repaired and reconditioned after bomb damage, in September 1947. The ill-fated king was not necessarily in principle a bad role for Guinness, but for a relatively young actor still finding his individual voice it was unfortunate that it was a role in which he was very likely to be over-influenced by one of his idols, John Gielgud. Guinness, had, after all, not only seen Gielgud's big commercial success in *Richard of Bordeaux* several times at a very impressionable age, but also he had played minor roles in Gielgud's company and under Gielgud's direction in this same Shakespeare play only ten years earlier, and had been able to watch the evolution of Gielgud's performance (definitive for many theatregoers) in this version of the role at very close quarters.

Consequently, it was a performance which never quite came out of the shadows. It is probable that without this experience in his theatrical past, Guinness would have arrived on his own accord at a very similar reading of the role to Gielgud's. But he would have done it unselfconsciously. As it was, there was always a sense of constraint about his reading, as though he did not want to be accused (most of

ABOVE: Ralph Richardson directs Guinness and Renée Asherson in Richard II.

LEFT: the aesthete-king Richard II.

all by himself) of aping Gielgud, but could not manage to come up with a completely independent version: he was like Gielgud in the role, but with most of the distinguishing features removed. Of course, he was not exactly aided by an inexperienced director (Richardson), nor, for that matter, by a very complex and unworkable permanent set, devised by Michael Warre according to Richardson's obscure and oracular pronouncements. Defenders of Guinness's playing (and they were not lacking) found the impersonality, the preservation of a critical distance which Brecht had not yet taught us to call alienation, to be the most interesting, positive contribution: the rest were disturbed by the pervading chill, the failure of the performance to take fire and be other than intelligent and distant.

Fortunately this was not Guinness's only leading role with the company that season: if, the previous season, he was being unobtrusively groomed for stardom, this season he had clearly made it. In Gogol's *The Government Inspector* he played the central role of the nobody who is mistaken for an important emissary from the government to this one-horse Russian town and sees soon enough how to profit from the locals' error. It was a role he could play well: a little man who can become big only when securely disguised behind a mask. His comic timing was duly admired: for the first time specific comment was made on his most specific talent – that of letting us see a mind working. As Hlestakov gradually works out the implications of the situation in which he finds himself, and, though no genius himself, discovers that at least he is quicker-witted than the numbskulls all round him, the dawn of his delight, the glee with which he tries out just how far he can go too far, were wondrously conveyed.

The 'Inspector' arrives: Guinness as Hlestakov in The Government Inspector.

Even better was his performance as the Dauphin in Shaw's *Saint Joan*. It is of course a character who could qualify as something of a wise fool, such as Guinness had played so tellingly before in Shakespeare. Critics were not slow to notice again the slight physical resemblance, no doubt deliberately emphasised in the makeup, to Stan Laurel, and Guinness gained praise for his evident relation, physical and emotional, to the great clowning tradition out of the commedia dell'arte – a touch of the Pagliacci has always been a sure way to British critics' hearts. Especially since the Joan of Celia Johnson was generally considered too slight and fey for Shaw's level-headed, big-boned country girl, and so, exceptionally, more attention was thrown on to the Dauphin and most of the reviews came his way.

Anyone who had followed Guinness's career attentively would not be entirely surprised by these performances, since they were clearly related to what he had played before and played well. The fourth pro-

LEFT: *as the Dauphin, with Celia Johnson as St Joan* AND ABOVE: *Guinness wore one of his more elaborate false noses as the Dauphin.*

duction of the season, *Coriolanus*, brought in something new, though something which retrospectively we can see as another Guinness speciality emergent. His Menenius, the man between the dictator Coriolanus and the Roman people, is the first of his memorable old men. Menenius is a strong man suffering only from the physical infirmities of age, subtle and intelligent though he seems to fumble, and Guinness, in one of his more striking physical transformations, captured exactly the man's rather stiff-necked quality, the pride and firmness of purpose beneath the frailty. It is not a role in which an actor would normally be expected to run away with all the best notices, but Guinness did, quite fairly, and by the end of this Old Vic season there was no doubt that a new star was out in the theatrical firmament.

But what sort of a star? Of the then 'big five' he resembled Gielgud most in his sensitivity and Michael Redgrave in his intelli-

As Shakespeare's elder statesman Menenius in Coriolanus.

gence. But he was not a 'new Gielgud' or a 'new Redgrave', even supposing that either were deemed necessary. In any case it was easy to pick out in advance a typical Gielgud or Richardson or Redgrave or Wolfit role, and though they were not necessarily confined to this sort of typecasting, one always knew just what face was behind the mask. Even Olivier, the most deliberately various of the greats, could be recognised by a certain directness which told one that even his Hamlet could not be a dreamer, but had to be a man of action, albeit contradictory action. But Guinness? What was his face really like? Though he was now playing the star roles, had he that not precisely definable unity behind the diversity, that gift for making all the faces his own instead of refashioning his own face unrecognisably into whatever was required?

His own answer to these questions would have been characteristically ambiguous. He had not, in his own mind, been tempted to confuse the work of an actor with that of a mimic ever since, during his 1937–38 season with Gielgud's company, the senior actor Leon Quartermaine had caught him mimicking in the wings and had firmly told him that he had to choose which he was going to be. He recognised the justice of this and kept his keen sense of mimicry for private entertainment. On the other hand, he always felt that the great advantage of acting was that one could transform oneself at will, hiding the self one did not want to be beneath the semblance of another, not maybe preferable but at all events different. Here maybe he most resembled Olivier, another lover of stage disguises. But temperamentally they were poles apart. And that, finally, was what the public and the critics wanted, needed to know. What was the temperament which, like a subtle essence, permeated and animated all his characteristics? It was a puzzle, but if he was to remain in the spotlight of stardom an answer would of necessity be forthcoming.

Guinness at home in Hammersmith; (ABOVE) *with his wife Merula, and* (RIGHT) *in his workshop.*

Not just for the moment, however. When he finished the Old Vic season in May 1948 he turned aside from acting in the theatre for a few months to make two films which were to be of prime importance in creating and shaping his screen career, *Oliver Twist* and *Kind Hearts and Coronets*; his only work in the theatre during this time was his first directing job, staging *Twelfth Night* for the Old Vic at short notice, with a cast and sets already fixed before he was involved. Though he had himself played Sir Andrew Aguecheek with notable success in the play, one cannot help wondering whether Feste was the role he really coveted, he with his early predilection for sweet/sour clowns. At any rate, in this production Feste became a principal character, involved in every aspect of the action, secretly in love with Olivia and aware of everything else that was going on in this sad comedy of multiple disguises and deceptions. Robert Eddison was directed – or wisely took the hint – to play the jester much as Guinness might have, and the overall result was interesting, if rather bizarre.

All things considered, Guinness had not had a very fair deal with

his directing debut. But the films more than made up for that. They gave him every opportunity to back, as it were, into the limelight, in that he played showy roles which importantly turned on his own mastery of disguise, his delight in makeup which would render him as nearly as possible unrecognisable. It might be questioned – and no doubt the ever self-critical Guinness asked the question himself many times – whether his playful/sinister Fagin in *Oliver Twist* or the eight members of the d'Ascoyne family in *Kind Hearts and Coronets* were finally more than clever pieces of mimicry. But on the whole they came over, against all odds, as something much more: virtuoso pieces surely, but with a virtuosity which did not draw attention to itself and demand applause on its own account. These were performances as well, and after publicity-inspired awe at the physical transformations had waned, the effect of the characterisations as characterisations remained uppermost in the mind.

Fagin, of course, presents a special problem. Even as it was, this presentation of a Jewish character as villainous caused angry reactions and attempts to have the film banned in America. But what does one do? As with Shylock, one may try to wrench Dickens' creation out of its period context altogether and present him as a victim, thereby changing the whole balance of the work. Or, as in more recent versions of *Oliver Twist* on film, one may play down the Jewish element and sanitise Fagin into a lovable rogue. Guinness (and Lean, evidently) chose neither of these get-outs, but instead gave us a character of truly Dickensian largeness and complexity. In one of his most elaborate disguises, Guinness was Fagin precisely as described by Dickens, accepting fully the hostile stereotype of the surface. But just

OLIVER TWIST

OPPOSITE: Guinness's elaborate makeup as Fagin; ABOVE: how it was done AND BELOW: David Lean directs a makeup session. Below left, Fagin directs a class in picking pockets, with Anthony Newley (RIGHT) as the Artful Dodger.

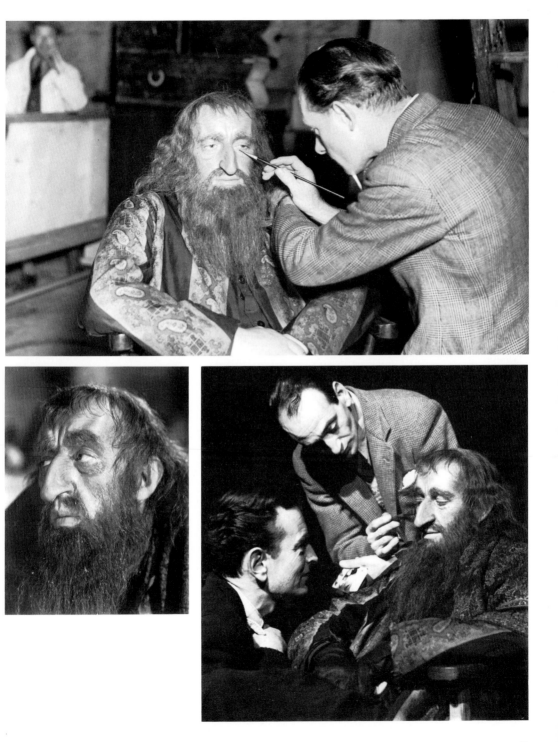

as Dickens could never diminish, but always tended to give everyone an heroic, larger-than-life dimension, so Fagin in Guinness's hands becomes a bizarre human being, with sympathetic elements inextricably mixed with unpleasant. He shows the way for subsequent players of the role, but none has been able to hold this delicate balance, forcing us to see Fagin as a complex individual from whom, like him or dislike him, no facile generalisations, racial or otherwise, can be inferred.

In *Oliver Twist* comedy and drama are completely intertwined; in *Kind Hearts and Coronets* high comedy rules. Or at first glance it does. It is only when you think about it afterwards that the serious side becomes apparent. Black comedy you can certainly say it is, but the blackness of this comedy of murders is no flip gesture. When Louis Mazzini determines to murder his way through his mother's insufferable family, who have rejected her and him, to a title and a fortune, it is a revolutionary gesture, even though it is all done with a patrician elegance out of Wilde. And for this gesture to have any meaning, the d'Ascoynes have to be, even within the comic convention, believable and, to a greater or lesser extent, monstrous. Any easy gallery of picturesque disguises would not do. And, to his infinite credit, this is not what Guinness provides.

No one seems to remember now exactly how the notion of his playing the whole family came about. At first the intention was to find eight different actors with a sufficient resemblance to play the family convincingly. Then at some point Guinness was offered three of the roles. He, it seems, thought this was rather silly: if three, why not all? And, in the end, that is how it was. Michael Balcon, producer-in-charge at Ealing Films, gave the idea his blessing, though in some ways it went against the traditional team spirit of the group, for however far Ealing Films might aspire to be a communal effort, he could not fail to be aware from his earlier career that a star could draw audiences in a way nothing else could. And already he recognised in Guinness the potentiality of film stardom.

Kind Hearts and Coronets was in other respects rather out of the Ealing routine. The studio's reputation – for already 'Ealing comedy' was well on the way to becoming a brand image – was for small-scale, cosy, defiantly British films: dramas and picturesque comedies which showed the British to themselves the way they wanted to be seen. It was largely coincidental when, as a result of films like *Passport to Pimlico, Whisky Galore* and *Kind Hearts and Coronets*, they became truly popular in the States and elsewhere in the world, simply demonstrating that with international audiences the best bet is to remain firmly and unflinchingly national. But *Kind Hearts and Coronets*, though as unequivocally English as any of them, fitted neither into the stereotype of cosiness and fundamental amiability nor into that of the group effort. For technical reasons it was made outside the family circle at Pinewood, and it was very definitely the creation of one man, the writer-director Robert Hamer. And the tone of epigrammatic

KIND HEARTS AND CORONETS

OVERLEAF, TOP LEFT: James Fitton's poster. TOP RIGHT: the Admiral insists on going down with his ship. BELOW: eight Guinnesses for the price of one – the d'Ascoyne family. OPPOSITE: Lady Agatha d'Ascoyne.

ruthlessness was in the tradition of Oscar Wilde but also that of such very British classics as Harry Graham's *Ruthless Rhymes for Heartless Homes*. Everyone remembers Louis disposing of the suffragette Lady Agatha with a bow-shot straight at her hot-air balloon and observing 'I shot an arrow in the air – she fell to earth in Berkeley Square', or comforting himself over a slight qualm at killing a good-time girl along with the young rake d'Ascoyne with the thought that during the weekend she had already no doubt suffered a fate worse than death.

Since, very properly, the devil gets all the best lines, Guinness is always on the receiving end of Louis's polite brutality. But it is amazing what a strong and vivid image of the English aristocracy he manages to conjure up from this series of quick sketches. And he is at his best, not with the obvious grotesques like the admiral who manages to sink his own ship from sheer stupid obstinacy or the general who is blown-up with some booby-trapped caviare while retelling for the hundredth time how he was personally responsible for the most disastrous engagement in the Boer War, but the more delicate portrayals, like the rather hen-pecked d'Ascoyne who engages in amateur photography partly at least so that he can take a quick drink in his potting-shed dark-room, or the more clearly dangerous duke with his passion for blood-sports. And the clerical d'Ascoyne, who could easily be no more than a broadly caricatured dodderer ('and I always say that my west window has all the exuberance of Chaucer, without, happily, any of the concomitant crudities...') comes to life as a grotesque but still believable human being – another in Guinness's long gallery of eccentric old gentlemen.

Describing working with Guinness, Robert Hamer, who was to work with him three more times, gave the impression that he was some sort of Method actor, entering so completely into his character that he continued to carry about with him the aura off-screen. If he was a good-time Charlie everyone was part of the fun, but if he was a senior lord you wanted to call him 'Sir'. This may well be true, to the outside observer, but Guinness himself has always taken the opposite view, even to risking the charge of mimicking rather than acting: he believes in starting with the outside and working in. Consequently his makeup for each d'Ascoyne was a crucial part in the individuation of the character – along with his observation of how such a person would talk and move. Once all that was right, the rest would follow naturally.

In *Kind Hearts and Coronets* it evidently did. When the film came out in mid-1949 there was no doubt about it: Guinness was a film star, though one would have been hard put to it to say what sort of star.

Not that definitions matter when public response is so unequivocal. For the moment, however, he was back on the stage, again in what was obviously a starring role, but this time the lead in a conventional West End production. All too conventional, as it turned out: *The Human Touch*, by J. Lee Thompson (subsequently to find greater fame as a film-maker on such films as *The Guns of Navarone*) and Dudley Leslie, was clearly meant to be a serious think-piece founded on fact, about James Simpson, a Scottish doctor who pioneered the use of chloroform as an anaesthetic, against all sorts of objections during the mid-nineteenth century. It was a respectable, rather dull piece which brought about the hero's final vindication by a good deal of implausible somersaulting in the attitudes of the opposition, got luke-warm notices and staggered on for about four months entirely on Guinness's presence in the cast – as sure a sign as any that he had arrived.

What he really needed, of course, was a role more inherently interesting than that of Simpson, or for that matter than Whimple,

LEFT: *as the crusading doctor James Simpson in* The Human Touch *with Sophie Stewart.*

ABOVE: Guinness wrestles with his editor (Clive Morton) in A Run For Your Money.

the gardening correspondent shaken out of his rut when he has to report on the doings of a lot of wild Welshmen up for the football in Ealing's minor comedy *A Run for Your Money*, which was his next offering. As always, Guinness's appearance in the role offers some small delights in its study of the prim and old-maidish Englishman just longing to find some way of letting his wilder emotions loose. (Observe, for instance, his reactions at the climactic rugby match when he cannot quite restrain himself from cheering on England.) But substandard Ealing could not be totally transfigured, only lit up a bit around the edges.

Happily, if coincidentally, the clinching role in the theatre was just round the corner. At the Edinburgh Festival in 1949 Guinness found

LEFT: as the mysterious psychiatrist Harcourt Reilly, Guinness disturbs Eileen Peel and Robert Flemyng in The Cocktail Party.

himself playing the enigmatic central character, Sir Henry Harcourt Reilly, in T.S. Eliot's new verse play *The Cocktail Party*, a role which in 1950 he was to take to New York, and was to do again, in a somewhat different fashion, in 1969. Harcourt Reilly is, suitably enough, a man of mystery, someone who, like Guinness himself, can be all things to all men. Before even the actor has anything to say about the role, Eliot himself is playing an elaborate game of concealments and disguises: what appears to be a smooth stranger intervening socially in the lives of a number of more or less discontented society people proves to be a fashionable psychiatrist and is eventually revealed as an emissary from another world. It comes as little surprise, finally, to learn that the play is a modern-dress variation on the *Alcestis* of Euripides, and that Harcourt Reilly owes a number of his superficial

RIGHT: Guinness brings his supernatural skills to bear on Cathleen Nesbitt in The Cocktail Party.

BELOW: Ronald Searle's Punch *caricature of Guinness and Robert Flemyng in* The Cocktail Party.

eccentricities to the fact that he is a Greek god in disguise. Guinness, with his chameleon-like presence on stage, proved triumphantly able to carry off the many unpredictable changes of tempo and mood in the piece: one moment he was the suave interloper, totally in control of the situation and making everyone else feel they should know what he is doing there, the next a slightly sinister elf, with his little enigmatic snatches of song and dance. The inscrutable dealer-out of divine intervention in human affairs with whom we end was equally central to his range – there has been no one better at withdrawing inside himself, beyond our power to reach him, before our very eyes.

For some reason Guinness did not play the role when the play opened in London. (Improbably, Rex Harrison played it instead.) But he had a great triumph with it in New York, effacing memories (if

any) of his brief stay on Broadway eight years earlier. And, coinciding as it did with the American release of *Kind Hearts and Coronets*, it laid the foundations for his continuing popularity in the United States. This was confirmed later in 1950 with his first appearance in a big Hollywood movie – for that is what *The Mudlark* was, though made in England. It is the kind of picturesque, American-eyed view of English royalty and aristocracy which in the 1930s would have been made entirely in the studio in Los Angeles, and would have provided work for a dozen or so of the 'Hollywood Raj'. Then, perhaps, George Arliss would have been called upon to do one of his renowned historical impersonations as Disraeli – the sort of thing Guinness imitated at his first drama-school auditions. But now it was Guinness himself, playing the role for real. The makeup, as ever, was ingenious and precise, and he made the most of his big speech in Parliament advocating social reform. There was not much to the rest of the film, however – it is a slight anecdote about an accidental meet-

BELOW: as the doomed hero of Last Holiday.

ing between a young Thames mudlark and the old queen when he somehow manages to penetrate Windsor Castle, and how it is used by Disraeli as a lever to urge the queen back into public life after her years of retirement and mourning for Prince Albert. Victoria is played by Irene Dunne to conform with rather sentimental American notions of her, and despite the British locations and predominantly British cast the film's American director (Jean Negulesco) and writer (Nunnally Johnson) give it a slick Hollywood finish which left the total effect somewhere uncomfortably mid-Atlantic. However, the film was a success on both sides of the Atlantic, was chosen for the Royal Film Performance that year, and won Guinness the *Picturegoer* Gold Medal as most popular actor.

An even clearer indication that his film career was taking off came from his other film of 1950, *Last Holiday*. This was completely British, modestly budgeted, and had no American stars to help sell it, and yet it actually had a greater commercial and critical success in the States than it did in Britain. It owed a lot to the original script by J. B. Priestley – a rather pat story of a man who is erroneously given only a few months to live by his doctor and determines to live them to the full, doing as many as possible of the things he has never had time or dared to do. The ending is characteristic Priestley, reminiscent of some of his pseudo-philosophical 'time plays', in that the preordained is, after all, preordained: when George Bird, on the brink of a success, social, financial and romantic, that he has never known before, receives his medical reprieve he is instantly killed another way, in a road accident: the Fates have decided that this shall be his 'last holiday' and that is just what it is bound to be. But whatever one might say about the too-easy irony of the script, it did at least give Guinness a fine opportunity to do what he could do best. The character is at the beginning a tabula rasa, the quintessence even of nothingness. But gradually he blossoms, takes on shape and colour, becomes a person. It was almost as though we were watching Guinness's creative process as an actor, seeing how the man without a face could little by little assume one. The film marked a new stage in Guinness's career in another way: it gave him his first undoubted starring role, and showed that, centre-screen, with everything depending on him, he could carry a film with ease.

The film career was not yet in danger of taking over completely. Indeed, in the following year Guinness was to take on the major theatrical challenge of providing what might be, and with any luck would be, his definitive, mature Hamlet. His first Hamlet had been a product of his youth, and was done in a deliberately experimental spirit – experimental for the director and the designer as much as for the principal actor. Then he had been twenty-four; now he was thirty-seven and should, for this role, be at the height of his powers. Unfortunately, it did not turn out quite that way. As it happens, we have what must be a unique blow-by-blow account of the production from a major theatre critic – unique because Kenneth Tynan was invited to make his only professional appearance on stage as the Player King. The circumstances could hardly have been more propitious. Guinness was given, by the producer Henry Sherek, carte blanche to put together something spectacularly worthy of the Festival of Britain. He had complete control of the casting, design and direction, which he undertook himself in collaboration with a young and theatrically untried director from the BBC, Frank Hauser.

It should have been the moment to emerge finally from the shadow of his illustrious forebears, particularly Gielgud, concerning whom Guinness admitted, in an article for *The Spectator* after his own production closed: 'When I came to play Hamlet for the first time, in 1938, in Guthrie's modern-dress production at the Old Vic, I was merely a pale shadow of Gielgud with some fustian Freudian trimmings...' Now it could be different, and so it was, but not very satisfactorily so. Tynan blames the production's failure on Guinness's own personal mixture of independence and humility: at once he needed to leave his own mark on the role and the production, and to respect the long theatrical tradition from which he sprang. In his own description, Guinness hoped that his attitude showed 'how an actor can react against the traditional and yet be steeped in it and love it'. But by eschewing both the 'heroics, struttings and bellowings' (his own words) of the old school of Shakespearean acting, and the modern tendency to underplaying, working towards a kind of psychological realism which also exists in Shakespeare, he set himself a task which might perhaps have been achieved only by someone with far more unselfcritical confidence in his own powers and judgment than Guinness ever had.

The result was a production plagued with indecision and sometimes downright perversity. Guinness had been convinced by Salvador de Madariaga's recent essay on Hamlet in only one respect – the argument that Spain was in Shakespeare's time as potent and pervasive an influence on the rest of the world as is the United States in our own time – and so he employed a Spanish designer, Mariano Andreu, but then gave him the impossible task of embodying a 'reaction against permanent, semi-permanent and realistic sets in Shakespeare'. As Tynan pertinently inquires, 'if you react against permanent, semi-permanent and realistic sets, what is there left to support?' Then the casting, principally from actors largely or entirely inexperienced in Shakespeare, edged over from the enterprising to the foolhardy – especially since the divided responsibility for direction tended to produce a situation in which each co-director demurely deferred to the other and no clear-cut decisions on the reading were ever taken.

All this might have been incidental and unimportant if Guinness's own Hamlet at the centre had been blazingly brilliant. But it wasn't. Almost all the decisions it reflected were, like those in the production in general, negative. Guinness knew, and his audiences clearly understood, what he did not want his Hamlet to be. But it was far from

OPPOSITE: Cecil Beaton's study of Guinness as Hamlet.

As Hamlet with Alan Webb as Polonius (LEFT).

clear what he did positively intend. And at this distance in time one cannot but ask how Guinness, the Guinness we knew and admired for some half-century, would, could and should have played the role in order to be true to himself and no pale reflection of anyone else. In his own comments on the role, Guinness pinpointed the chameleon-like character of Hamlet, and placed particular emphasis on his decision not to make the traditional break after 'Oh what a rogue and peasant slave am I…', so that instead, 'the audience was given that and then "To be or not to be" within a minute and a half, followed by the "nunnery" scene, followed by the social ease of "Speak the speech" – in fact, they get the greater part of Hamlet's character stripped bare before them…And all in the space of about fifteen minutes.'

So could his Hamlet have been a man of mystery and disguises, like Harcourt Reilly able to be all things to all men while keeping his own true nature (if anything so simple-sounding really existed) in reserve? Possibly. But this would presumably require a sense of purpose as steely as Harcourt Reilly's to be sensed beneath. Tynan describes just such a backbone to the character emerging sometimes in rehearsals – 'a touch of the headsman, judicious and inexorable' – but observed also that as rehearsals continued it was slowly ironed out. Clearly Guinness needed either to be single-handed director, or to be directed by someone experienced enough to take a strong line with him and the rest of the cast, leaving him only with the irreducible actor's responsibility for making sense of his own role. Instead, rehearsals drifted along rudderless, and the first night was a disaster, greeted with boos from the gallery. Guinness as usual blamed himself: after the final curtain he said to the company 'It was my fault. Don't blame yourselves. I gave up in the first act.' And having given up, he appears to have given up decisively: though a few excrescent details of production, such as a ludicrously expressionistic treatment of the play scene, were shorn after the first night, no further rehearsals were called to try and salvage the enterprise – it merely limped on as it was for another fifty-one performances, strongly defended by a few but greeted in luke-warm terms at best by most of the critics and the disappointed public.

It seems unlike him to give up so thoroughly. What about 'the show must go on' and all that – an important part of the tradition he so revered? It is well-known that in virtually all his major roles, and indeed major successes, Guinness got cold feet somewhere along the way, and begged and pleaded to be released from his contractual obligations. So much so that it became a ritual, not perhaps taken totally seriously even by himself. Though he was an Aries, he should have been a Virgo, since for him it had to be rape every time, with someone else taking final, formal responsibility. But this sort of throwing in the towel in the midst of the bout seems very different. And perhaps we would not be too far astray if we attributed it to the very real, and clearly excessive, humility of the man. Humility is all very well and admirable as a quality, but it can be overdone. Few actors seem inclined to overdo it, but Guinness was an exception to the rule. He never seemed to feel that 'Because that's what I want', or 'That's the way I see it' constitutes an adequate, acceptable answer to any of the important questions of life. But sometimes a star actor, let alone a director, has to have a touch of monomania in order to function: though talent helps, conviction and self-confidence are often nine-tenths of the game.

Also, it is interesting to consider the *Hamlet* debacle in relation to the whole pattern of Guinness's career, and in particular his singularity among Britain's great actors, or even among those aspiring to the title. Some oddities are obvious. As has been mentioned, he was extraordinary in having had virtually his entire stage career in London, with no provincial beginnings or subsequent attachments whatever. Also, though he never lost contact completely with the stage, the cinema was of more central importance to him, for more of his career, than it has to any of his peers. And while on the stage, he had less to do with the classics, or for that matter those great repositories of classical tradition, the National Theatre and the Royal Shakespeare Company, than any of the rest. Indeed, he quite frequently expressed his lack of interest in the classics, and even his determination never to act in a classic again. From his formative years, he was almost exclusively a West End stage actor, almost entirely in new plays. His forays into Shakespeare even, that touch-stone of classical acting, were few and far between. Presumably he must have sensed the challenge there, or he would not have done his 1951 Hamlet, or his 1966 Macbeth. But on the whole it was clearly a challenge he preferred not to take up. And this cannot have been only because both these major Shakespearean exercises were critical and financial disasters. It probably went deeper, to his humility and lack of self-confidence, which made him at once profoundly impression-able and agonisingly wary of trying to challenge the greats of earlier years or of his own time on what he conceived to be their home ground but not his. No one ever doubted his brilliance as a support-ing actor in Shakespeare. But it cannot be for nothing that all his attempts at a leading tragic role ended in disaster.

Perhaps this means that he became a modern actor in modern roles *faute de mieux*. But, even if so, his distinctive gift was uniquely to bring classic authority and awareness of tradition to modern roles in new plays, making the lounge suit as believable a garb for a tragic hero as doublet and hose. It is all part of the disguise syndrome: any-one who plays a major role in Shakespeare is automatically putting himself on the line in a certain way: Othello, say, may disguise the man radically, but it does not, cannot, disguise the actor, who is mak-ing a certain statement about himself even by undertaking the role. In any case, it is no way to go unrecognised, to back into the limelight. And if the approach was not devious or oblique, Guinness wished to have none of it.

That seems like a rather paradoxical way to describe the film work which was coming to occupy more and more of his time, but it is finally not inaccurate. The 'Ealing comedies' with which Guinness was becoming increasingly identified at this stage of his career were, after all, famed primarily for their directness, one might almost say their artlessness. They carefully avoided anything that could be read as sophistication (*Kind Hearts and Coronets* remaining always the exception that proved the rule); they were popular entertainment for a mass audience, and with their healthy, extrovert air of group endeavour they discouraged all notions of the film as complex per-sonal expression of the artist as individual. But within this self-consciously simplistic context, Guinness's contribution proves on examination to be as intricate and evasive as one can possibly conceive.

FILM STAR

Though Guinness was now a star on both stage and screen, the nature of his stardom in films was rather different. In films, especially films like the Ealing comedies, with their mistrust of all star nonsense, it is perfectly possible to be a star character actor. This, for some years, Guinness was: he very seldom played roles which are close to the essence of normal screen stardom in that they are based fairly and squarely on the actor's own personality. Cary Grant, say, brilliant acting technician as he always was, never played a role in which he was not recognisable as Cary Grant, and indeed this ready recognition was always a vital part of the role's effect: no film-maker would see much point in casting Cary Grant in a wildly divergent role, and the public would see little point in a Cary Grant they could not recognise. With Guinness, on the other hand, the interest was more usually in the role, and the ability of the performer to make you forget something you already know: you are so absorbed in the character that you virtually forget who is playing it.

In that light, Guinness's performance in his next Ealing comedy, *The Lavender Hill Mob*, can be seen as starring only in the formal sense that he got top billing and played the principal role. He was not even in a heavy physical disguise: only a pair of prim metal-rimmed spectacles to emphasize the servile, dutiful, rather old-maidish nature of Henry Holland, the quiet clerk who oversees deliveries of gold bullion to the Bank of England with precision and an unquestioning sense of duty. But the psychological transformation was complete: even if Guinness took the film very lightly, as just a romp, audience belief in the character was nonetheless complete and vital to the film's effect. Like a number of the other films made at Ealing around this time, *The Lavender Hill Mob* celebrated a sort of whimsical triumph of the little man, the worm who finally turns or the ordinary who suddenly turns out to be extraordinary. The model bank clerk is inspired to rebellion by a fellow inmate of his suburban boarding house (Stanley Holloway), when between them they come up with a plan to steal a load of gold and, more important, secrete it satisfactorily to get it out of the country by means of a business manufacturing cheap models of the Eiffel Tower as tourist souvenirs – for who will notice if the consignment is actually made of gold? The comedy of this situation, and of Guinness's performance, is sustained and enhanced by the perfect gravity with which the argument is developed from this fantastical premise: Henry Holland may be having fun for the first time in his life, but his character is conceived and presented with never less than total seriousness.

The Man in the White Suit, Guinness's other Ealing comedy of 1951, is rather different – more pretentious and finally, I think, less satisfactory. Partly this may be because Guinness's real face and, as we may suppose, nature are less disguised here than in any other of his Ealing films, and partly because the script basis of the film proposes a situation which it then cannot satisfactorily resolve. This time the hero is properly so called: he is heroic in much the same way as the

PREVIOUS PAGE: The Man in the White Suit adopts a crusading stance.

THE LAVENDER HILL MOB
BELOW: Ronald Searle's poster.

OPPOSITE, TOP: Guinness and Stanley Holloway on location in Paris.

BELOW: Guinness inspects Stanley Holloway's stock-in-trade of tourist souvenirs.

THE MAN IN THE WHITE SUIT
OPPOSITE: the idealistic inventor begins to feel beleaguered.

RIGHT: teabreak during the shooting.

Mr Deeds who went to town or the Mr Smith who went to Washington. That is, he is a young and attractive idealist who sets out to benefit the world, a little man who gets big by trying. The only difference between Alexander Mackendrick's comedy and Frank Capra's is that while Capra's hardboiled world always proved to have a soft centre, so that goodwill prevailed, Mackendrick's is much more seriously unready for Sidney Stratton, the unworldly scientist bent on discovering the indestructible, undirtiable white cloth. And with reason: it is not only evil big business that is against him when he appears to have discovered it, but finally everybody, even the littlest people who see themselves put out of their jobs as the manufacture and cleaning of cloth phases itself out for ever. A bitter truth – and quite possibly too bitter to embody in a cosy Ealing comedy.

Certainly the film seems finally to be torn apart on the horns of its own dilemma: in the nick of time the white cloth proves unstable and dissolves, and its inventor is cruelly mocked before going off to continue his search and to do better next time. But why, and for whom? A man with a mission becomes merely a man with a mania, and so hardly comprehensible as a little-man hero at all. And though the film was immensely successful, one of those that made Guinness as famous as the Ealing trademark under which he worked, this does not seem in retrospect one of his more successful performances. Partly no doubt it is the way the character is written: apart from the unworldly idealism, we never really know what makes Sidney tick, and left without any noticeable physical or psychological disguise Guinness does not manage to invest him with much more than a shy, slightly idiot charm. Though in commercial terms one of his most successful performances, it remains one of his least interesting from this era.

Had the *Hamlet* achieved some kind of clinching success, Guinness's career might have taken on a very different shape. He had plans to follow it immediately by playing King Magnus in Shaw's *The*

Apple Cart, and then to star on stage with one or other of his long-standing idols, Tallulah Bankhead and Edwige Feuillère. But the collapse of *Hamlet* naturally drove him back to the screen, where, though he was no more personally secure, he was being actively sought-after to follow up the Ealing successes now on release. For his new film in 1951 he had the sense to choose a role which required him to be very different from his diffident private self: Arnold Bennett's 'card' Denry Machin, a cheery and shameless opportunist whose sheer cheek carries him almost effortlessly to the top of local society, from school cheat to mayor in a few easy lessons. As always, Guinness had got the stance, the walk and the accent off to perfection, and clearly revelled in playing the sort of person that most of his screen characters would only, guiltily and ineffectually, dream of being. He even, wonder of wonders, got the girl and the other woman. And the film continued his string of successes, both in Britain and in America, where it was called *The Promoter*, as the original title, *The Card*, was regarded as incomprehensible. It was directed by Ronald Neame, whom Guinness had first encountered as David Lean's producer and

LEFT: *as Arnold Bennett's 'Card' in an improbably heroic moment, after helping rescue the shipwrecked in* The Card.

script collaborator on *Great Expectations*, and who was to play an important part in Guinness's subsequent film career, second only, perhaps, to Lean himself.

It would have been understandable if the trauma of *Hamlet* had turned Guinness right away from the stage for some time. But obviously he was made of sterner stuff and bounced right back less than a year later with a highly contrasted vehicle, *Under the Sycamore Tree*, by Sam and Bella Spewack, which opened at the Aldwych Theatre in April 1952. He must have felt considerably more secure in this, since it was a new play, releasing him from his ambiguous relationship with theatrical tradition. It was directed by Peter Glenville, one of his small group of close personal friends, and offered him a role which made full use of his protean capacity for disguise and game-playing.

BELOW: Ronald Searle's Punch *caricature of Diana Churchill, Daphne Anderson, Guinness and Ernest Thesiger in* Under the Sycamore Tree, *AND RIGHT: an autographed programme.*

In other respects, though, it could hardly be said to be playing safe on his part – certainly not given the eccentricity of the play's premise: all the characters are ants, and Guinness was the Ant Scientist who has found out enough about the so-dissimilar (or is it?) world of men beyond the anthill to teach his fellow ants how to match mankind in

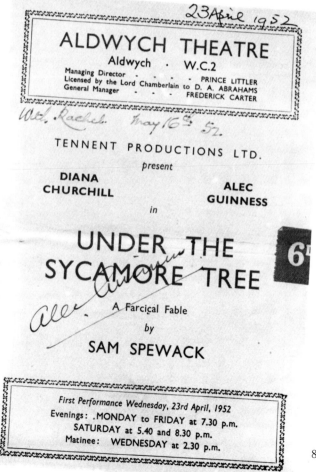

23 April 1952

ALDWYCH THEATRE
Aldwych · W.C.2
Managing Director - - - PRINCE LITTLER
Licensed by the Lord Chamberlain to D. A. ABRAHAMS
General Manager - - - FREDERICK CARTER

Wd. Rachel. May 16th 52.

TENNENT PRODUCTIONS LTD.
present

DIANA
CHURCHILL

ALEC
GUINNESS

in

UNDER THE
SYCAMORE TREE

6'

A Farcical Fable

by

SAM SPEWACK

First Performance Wednesday, 23rd April, 1952
Evenings: .MONDAY to FRIDAY at 7.30 p.m.
SATURDAY at 5.40 and 8.30 p.m.
Matinee: WEDNESDAY at 2.30 p.m.

LEFT: as the Ant Scientist in Under the Sycamore Tree.

communication and mechanisation, as well as how to fight among themselves with man's own weapons, like DDT.

Perhaps fortunately, the characters only talked like insects, but were not dressed that way: though they might talk of six legs they manifested only two. This rendered the old satirical parallel between mankind and the beastly world all the more evident, for anyone to whom this particular literary ploy might come as a puzzling novelty. In any case the play never managed to move much beyond a loosely assembled succession of revue sketches and one-liners, failing to assume the dimensions of coherent symbolic fable as its most famous predecessor, *The Insect Play* by Karel and Josef Capek (1921), had done. But at least it gave Guinness a field-day, dominating every scene as the infinitely guileful and adaptable ant intellectual and even aging to ninety in the last scene, for which, in looks at any rate, he did the best version of his renowned impersonation of Alistair Sim.

Though the play was not exactly a runaway success, Guinness got

OPPOSITE, TOP: shooting Malta Story *on location – Guinness and Muriel Pavlow embrace, Brian Desmond Hurst directs.*

BELOW: Malta Story *– a romantic juvenile at last.*

good notices and was generally enjoyed, which restored his theatrical confidence somewhat. Possibly it was in this agreeable frame of mind that he undertook to make his next film, and arguably least interesting ever, *Malta Story*. It is difficult to imagine why else he should have been tempted by the colourless role of a stiff-upper-lip English air-force pilot on Malta during the war. It is said that Guinness always fancied himself as a tragedian and accepted his general association with comedy at best unwillingly. Maybe, by the same token, he always hankered, just a little bit, to play a straightforward romantic lead rather than a gallery of eccentrics. (At the time of *Kind Hearts and Coronets* he said that he really longed to be a straight juvenile – 'Well, *almost* juvenile'.) If so, then at least *Malta Story* must have exorcised that particular demon for ever: he never looked more like the faceless man of his popular (and to him mystifying) reputation than here, when obviously what was needed to bulk out a dull role in a dull script was simply an exercise in big-star charisma, rather than a serious and detailed piece of character delineation.

The Captain's Paradise, which also took Guinness back to sunny Mediterranean locations, had the advantage of putting a perhaps not much more interesting character into a far more interesting situation. The constituents of the paradise are a wife, if not in every port, at least in the two essential ports, Gibraltar and the North African coast, between which Guinness's captain plies a steamer regularly. The Gibraltar wife (Celia Johnson) is staid and respectable and very English, while the North African wife (Yvonne De Carlo) is the perfect mistress-figure, providing for the colourful, fun side of his life. The fundamental truth, which the captain uncomfortably finds out in the course of the story, is of course that each secretly longs to be the other – the Latin temptress would like to be a solid housewife, while the solid housewife would love to run wild. Guinness does not have very much to do but register increasing alarm as his paradise falls farcically apart, but the film was popular and, suitably trimmed in length, showed widely in the States and helped to enhance his growing transatlantic reputation.

Some intriguing prospects were in the offing for Guinness at this time. An idea was floated that he should appear in a film of D.H. Lawrence's *Sons and Lovers* with Montgomery Clift, but nothing came of it. More immediately, he was asked to play the hero and solitary rebel against totalitarianism, Winston Smith, in a television adaptation of Orwell's *1984* for the BBC. It would have been

BELOW: Sherriffs caricature of Guinness and Celia Johnson running wild in The Captain's Paradise; *Guinness and his other wife (Yvonne de Carlo) on the dance floor.*

RIGHT: *Guinness as the crippled King of France in* All's Well That Ends Well, *with Irene Worth as Helena.*

admirable casting, and he was tempted, but he had already agreed to go out to Stratford, Ontario, in the summer of 1953 to star with Irene Worth (with whom he had worked most recently in *The Cocktail Party*) in the opening season of the new Shakespeare Playhouse there, thus inaugurating the annual Shakespeare festival which continues up to the present. As well as being an obvious honour and sign of transatlantic confidence, this plan also had the advantage of easing him back again into Shakespeare after the troubles with *Hamlet* , which might well have put him off for good. As it happens, his Canadian appearances as Richard III and the King of France in *All's Well That Ends Well* under Tyrone Guthrie's direction (the latter again in modern dress with the King confined to a wheelchair) did not – though satisfactorily, indeed enthusiastically, received – make any noticeable difference to his subsequent career, in which he only once made any important attempt to come to terms with Shakespeare again. But at least they made it clear that he was not just chickening out after a major defeat.

1953 was also lucky for him in that it brought him, on screen, one of those roles he was obviously born to play, G.K. Chesterton's whimsical priest-detective Father Brown. The idea and adaptation were Robert Hamer's, and the combination of Hamer's and Guinness's talents and personalities worked almost as well as in *Kind Hearts and Coronets*. Hamer, one of the rare true sophisticates of the British cin-

Opposite: Guinness as Richard III at Stratford, Ontario.

ema, cunningly devised a script with elements of several Father Brown stories, but centred on the slow drawing-in of the thread which the Roman Catholic Chesterton believed always attached a lapsed Catholic, however loosely and distantly, to the faith of his childhood. In this case it is the master thief Flambeau (Peter Finch) who is to be saved and brought back in the very process of Father Brown's retrieving the valuable cross Flambeau has stolen from the Church. But if this sounds rather heavy matter for a light-comedy detective yarn not so far away from Agatha Christie-land, the lightness and charm of the treatment rapidly dispel any lingering suspicion of pretentiousness and Guinness, twinkling quietly behind his steel-rimmed glasses, was seldom more happily or suitably used.

Oddly enough, Guinness was to go on immediately to play another, very different priest, this time a fictional cardinal (clearly suggested by Cardinal Mindzenty) imprisoned in a totalitarian state in Bridget Boland's tense drama, *The Prisoner*, which he played first on stage at the Globe Theatre in 1954 and then in a very close film adaptation on screen in 1955. Even odder, and not perhaps entirely coincidentally, in 1956 one of the most important external happen-

Right: Guinness as G.K. Chesterton's priest-detective Father Brown.

The Prisoner *on stage.* OPPOSITE: *the imprisoned cardinal,* AND ABOVE, *the beginning of the interrogation, with Noel Willman as the interrogator.*

ings of his life took place, when, after a period of instruction, he was formally received into the Roman Catholic Church. It is impossible to say - Guinness himself always found it impossible to say – what influence playing these two priestly roles, and the research necessary for them, may have had on this carefully meditated decision, but it seems likely that he could not have spent so much time in *The Prisoner*, an unmistakably serious and deeply felt piece, without being driven to some equally serious personal reappraisals.

The Prisoner is in certain respects a variation on the *Crime and Punishment* pattern: the cardinal enters prison affirming confidently that any confession he may be quoted as having made will be a lie or a product of human weakness. In fact, that may be literally true, for his torture is psychological rather than physical, a process by which he himself is driven to examine his conscience and the basic reasons for his actions and attitudes far more damagingly than any outside

agent could possibly do. He gradually, prodded and subtly directed by his interrogator, discovers that all his pride and his courage come from a deep-rooted sense of his own guilt and unworthiness: he blames himself for never having really loved his brother as himself, never really rejoiced in or responded to God. In fact his own humility and belief in his own inadequacy are the most potent forces working against him, and his ultimate breakdown and self-accusations at his show trial are all the result of it, carried under strain to neurotic excess – the sort of psychological situation in which he will even tell lies to make his condemnation more complete. And his punishment is the worst possible: no apparent punishment at all, but merely release on medical grounds to face again the world he claims to have betrayed.

    The role, coming in the middle of a lot of film comedies, seemed, especially in the film version (directed by Guinness's friend Peter Glenville), like a violent change of pace. But in fact it drew on what we would nowadays recognise as the central and most distinctive qualities of Guinness's talent – his ability to suggest thought, to convince us that his characters have an interior as well as an exterior life, and that intellect is in no way incompatible with humanity. His cardi-

The Prisoner *on film.* ABOVE: *the cardinal at the end of his tether.*

OPPOSITE: *cardinal and interrogator (Jack Hawkins).*

nal is clearly a man for whom the intellectual life is all, and yet he is none the less a human being for all that, and in certain respects a touchingly fallible human being, just because his intellect gives him no adequate defence against the promptings of his subconscious, his emotions and his instincts. And finally the cardinal is in many senses the victor, for his personality and his determination to carry self-examination to the brink, if necessary, of self-destruction have worked so powerfully on his interrogator, the instigator and observer of his deterioration, as to produce a respect and admiration which render him incapable of continuing in his old unquestioning faith in the Party and the rightness of things as they are. The play is not as profound as it perhaps ought to be: it is a work of popularisation, making comprehensible to a wide general audience matters which are essentially rarified and obscure. But it works admirably in those terms, and Guinness's gravitas manages to impart to it an air of possessing those depths which, on cool consideration, it really lacks.

The play was, relatively speaking, a popular success; the film was clearly a labour of love for all concerned, and rather puzzled Guinness's cinema audience, though by this time his name alone was sufficient to ensure it respectful attention. The film he made between stage and screen versions, another comedy with Robert Hamer called *To Paris With Love*, was a disappointment all round: his disguise as the sophisticated father of a grown-up son who is to be introduced to the romantic delights of Gay Paree is immaculate, but the farcical goings-on as each tries to push the other into a suitable affair with a suitable lady are a waste of everybody's time. Still, the world could breathe a sigh of relief when, immediately after the film of *The Prisoner*, one of the most famous and successful of all Guinness's Ealing comedies appeared. This was *The Ladykillers*, directed by the same Alexander Mackendrick who had been responsible for *The Man in the White Suit*.

Though it was, in commercial and critical terms, a peak in the careers both of Ealing and Guinness personally, *The Ladykillers* does not now seem to be much more than a marking-time for both. Guinness plays the leader of a gang of improbable and grotesque crooks whose activities centre on a suburban boarding-house run by a sweetly indestructible old lady (Katie Johnson) who keeps, quite unconsciously, throwing spanners into the works of their criminal

LEFT: *a normally staid Guinness gets into the spirit of Paris in* To Paris With Love.

ABOVE: the sinister Professor Marcus prepares his next crime in The Ladykillers.

organisation. The film is more a collection of quaint gags than a coherent story, and Guinness's own characterisation seems to depend much more heavily than usual on the physical make-up: Professor Marcus is an outrageously sinister figure with receding hair and jutting teeth who carries more than a momentary suggestion of that other 'man of a thousand faces' Lon Chaney in *The Phantom of the Opera*. The disguise is very effective, but, exceptionally with Guinness, one is left really with no idea what sort of person hides behind the disguise. At the time Guinness, or at any rate his appearance, was frequently compared with Alistair Sim; looking back, it is more interesting to observe him in the same frame as a young Peter Sellers (one of the gang), whose protean adaptability and gifts of disguise were soon to be very regularly compared with Guinness's own. Peter Sellers was later on in his career to run into precisely the same problem as Guinness: that of moving from the character-acting periphery to the starring centre of a film, and doing so with total conviction. If he never managed to solve the problem with such conviction and grace as Guinness, it may well have been merely because he was not vouchsafed so much time to come to terms with his own ego.

Actually, the actor's ego seems to have been the least of Guinness's problems, at any time in his career – unless one counts his constantly-aired self-doubts as a perverse manifestation. And in 1955 he had every reason to feel more than usual confidence. He was awarded a CBE. He had hits on stage and screen to his recent credit. He was besieged with tempting professional offers, most notably a suggestion by Alexander Korda that he should star in a big-budget film production of Shaw's *Arms and the Man*, where the playful, anti-heroic hero Bluntschli should have suited his gifts perfectly. (Sadly, Korda's death put a stop to the plan.) He had finally taken the plunge and moved from the house in the rundown Hammersmith square to his very own permanent home in the country, a discreetly modern house designed by his wife's brother which has been cheerfully described as 'the architectural scandal of Hampshire', just outside Petersfield, with enough land around it to repel the casually curious and allow him, until the 1980s, to list this address in all the Who's-Whos without apparent fear of too much intrusion on his privacy. He was accepted without question as one of the leaders of his profession: if any further demonstration of that was required, it could easily be seen from his placing in the 1954 RADA jubilee show, alongside everybody who was anybody, playing Sir Peter Teazle opposite Vivien Leigh as Lady Teazle in an extract from *The School for Scandal*. He was, moreover, just about to go into one of his biggest stage successes, Peter Glenville's adaptation of a Feydeau farce, *Hotel Paradiso*, at the Winter Garden, which, ten years later, he and Glenville would film together. And after that, the start of his international film career with his first Hollywood film, *The Swan*.

But, most important of all in his personal life, there was his con-

THE LADYKILLERS

ABOVE: Guinness and Danny Green dispose of the body.

LEFT: a quiet musical evening with Guinness, Peter Sellers and Herbert Lom (violins), Cecil Parker (viola) and Danny Green (cello).

OPPOSITE: Hotel Paradiso *on screen (ABOVE) with Peggy Mount, and on stage (BELOW) with Irene Worth. The theatre programme was designed by Osbert Lancaster.*

version to Roman Catholicism. For such a reticent man, Guinness was willing to talk surprisingly freely of the role assumed by religion in his life. For some years it was not very important to him. He was brought up with a conventional, semi-detached relationship to the Church of England, and during his teens went through, like most bright children, a period of reaction against religion of all kinds. As a young man he was even, by his own account, violently atheistic and

As Sir Peter Teazle, with Vivien Leigh as Lady Teazle, in a scene from The School for Scandal *in the RADA Jubilee celebration.*

anti-clerical. He seems, though, to have felt a recurrent need for some kind of religious or philosophical substructure to his life. Just before the war he recollected becoming interested in Buddhism and its possibilities. He read up quite a bit, then went to an actual Buddhist centre in South London for further guidance, only to be told that the holy man had left for the duration as he did not approve of the possibility of bombing. This did not seem to Guinness to suggest the

In church with his wife at a special mass for Pope John XXIII.

kind of faith he hoped to find, and so he effectively crossed Buddhism off his list.

It is recorded that he was very much affected by his first personal contact with the Pope, in Italy in 1945: he wrote to his friend Sir Sydney Cockerell 'I was deeply impressed by the Pope's personality. I felt that for the first time in my life I had seen a saint.' During the early 1950s he had started what was to be a lifelong habit of taking brief retreats in religious retreat houses, not necessarily for precisely defined religious purposes, but simply to cut himself off from the world for a while and clear his mind. Finally, in 1955, he decided secretly to take instruction, with the intention of being received into the Roman Catholic church. Six months before he himself was received, his son Matthew, then aged fifteen, preceded him; for the time being his wife did not do likewise, but then a year or so later, while he was on location for *The Bridge on the River Kwai*, she wrote to him to say that she too had been received, thus strengthening the unity of this always closely united family.

Guinness often spoke of an uncomfortable void in the centre of his life. Whether his religious beliefs were sufficient to fill this completely is a moot point. But at least in Roman Catholicism he seemed to have found something which brought him a certain tranquillity, in which his intellect and his instinct could be satisfactorily held in balance. It seems highly appropriate that though he took some two years of thought and study to convince himself, the first step on the road to belief was purely instinctive. He once told an interviewer that the turning point came when he was making *Father Brown* in France, near Macon, and one night was walking back to his lodgings still wearing his priest's costume: 'It was absolutely dark. I heard little footsteps running after me. Suddenly I felt my hand taken by a seven year-old boy, who walked with me all the way back to the village swinging my hand and chattering. I only caught little bits of what he was saying. I didn't dare utter a word in case I frightened him with a foreign accent or my clumsy French. I remained absolutely silent, and eventually he squeezed my hand and disappeared, and I thought it was simply marvellous that a child in the kind of dark, in a dark lane, will run up to a man because he's dressed as a priest. And it totally changed my attitude...I don't base my religion on that. But it's the attitude. No, I think it's marvellous that a small boy has confidence...I've always looked back on it as a magic moment...'

THE INTERNATIONAL YEARS

TIME

THE WEEKLY NEW

ACTOR
ALEC GUINNESS

When Alec Guinness finally went to Hollywood, it was for no very special reason. Or perhaps it was for all too special a reason: to play one of those important but unappealing roles for which it is generally felt a visiting 'actor', by definition not a star, would be ideal casting. The occasion was the filming of Molnar's play *The Swan*, previously made as Lillian Gish's first talkie in 1930. It was to be the last film made by Grace Kelly before her retirement from the screen to marry Prince Rainier of Monaco, and the choice of a romantic comedy with a royal marriage as the subject can hardly have been entirely coincidental. All the same, the details of the story, if closely examined, were not very appropriate, for this play concerns a princess who has a moment of romantic awakening with a handsome tutor in the royal household before finally choosing to marry her prince as a matter of duty. Obviously this situation required the tutor to be the attractive romantic lead, and the prince, though he finally gets the girl, to be a far less appealing, though not actually a repulsive figure. Hence the casting of Louis Jourdan as the tutor. And hence the doubts which might have been felt about whatever future career in Hollywood might result from Guinness's casting as the mature, chilly and correct prince.

Few doubted that Guinness gave an excellent performance. But it was an actor's performance, not a star's – and a particularly tough, unsentimental one at that. There is no attempt to rival the other male lead in charm or looks: the prince is a man who recognises his duty and his fate, and reads the princess correctly enough to know that she will ultimately do the same. He is clearly not displeased, on a personal level, that the princess chooses him rather than passionate escape – but he is never in any doubt that her choice of him, inevitable as it is, has little or nothing to do with his own charms. We may observe that he is a pleasant enough man, and the marriage may well turn out to be happy – happier at any rate than love in a hut with the tutor. But it is never in any way presented as a choice in accordance with romantic fantasy on the subject. Knowing Guinness as we do, we are not surprised that he makes no attempt to pull the text out of shape by winks and nudges and sly twinkles at the camera to indicate that really, whatever everything he does and says may tell us, he is really every princess's dream lover. It is a brave tactic, but not one which suggests future Hollywood stardom – or even any noticeable desire for it.

ABOVE: Guinness in 1982 with Lillian Gish, who starred in the first film version of The Swan.

That, no doubt, is about right. Guinness could hardly be expected to resist such a tempting invitation, and there seems no reason to suppose that he did this one just for the money, as he disarmingly admitted of some later Hollywood disasters, such as *Majority of One*. But he can certainly not have been planning on a long stay in Southern California. This feeling, if he had it, might well have been intensified by one of the strangest experiences of his life, his unaccountable premonition of James Dean's death. As he told it:

'On my very first night in Hollywood I met James Dean. It was a

PREVIOUS PAGE: Guinness makes the cover of Time – *drawing by Ben Shahn.*

The Swan: *Guinness with his royal fiancée's family (Jessie Royce Landis, Estelle Winwood, Brian Aherne).*

very odd occurrence. I had arrived off the plane, and I'd been met by Grace Kelly and various people, but I found that I was alone for the evening, and a woman I knew telephoned me and asked me out to dinner...We finally went into a little Italian dive and that was full, so we were turned away. Then I heard feet running down the street, and it was James Dean. He said, "I was in that restaurant when you couldn't get a table and my name is James Dean." He asked us to join him and then going back into the restaurant he said, "Oh, before we go in I must show you something – I've got a new car", and there it was in the courtyard of this little restaurant, some little silver car, very smart, all done up in cellophane and a bunch of roses tied to its bonnet, and I said, "How fast can you drive this?" and he said "Oh, I can only do 150 mph in it." I asked if he had driven it, and he replied that he had never been in it at all. Some strange thing came over me, some almost different voice and I said, "Look, I won't join your table unless you want me to, but I must say something, please do not get into that car because if you do (and I looked at my watch), it's now Thursday (whatever the date was) ten o'clock at night, and by ten o'clock at night next Thursday you'll be dead if you get into that car." I don't know what it was – nonsense, so we had dinner. We had a charming dinner, and he was dead the following Thursday afternoon in that car.'

In any case, immediately after completing his role in *The Swan* he went straight back to Britain to appear on the London stage in *Hotel Paradiso*. There, or about there, his international film career might have stayed, if it had not been for the happy chance of his being offered one of the three leads – in many ways the most important, but clearly the least appealing – in David Lean's film of Pierre Boule's novel *The Bridge on the River Kwai*.

Like many pieces of casting which, once done, seem inevitable and inconceivable any different, the assignment of Colonel Nicholson's role to Guinness happened largely by chance and was by no means foregone. It seems that Lean's first choice for it was Charles Laughton – perhaps on the basis of some faint relationship between the character of the martinet – though not sadist – Nicholson and the martinet Captain Bligh. When that casting proved impractical, the role was offered to Noël Coward, and though the casting sounds at first extremely improbable, the result might well have been extraordinarily interesting, something like the captain in *In Which We Serve* with delusions of grandeur or religious mania. Guinness was at best third choice, and when he was shown an early draft of the script turned it down flat, doubtful that any actor could make this blind fanatic interesting and in any way engaging of audience sympathies – let alone that he personally could do it. It was only after the script had been significantly revised and Lean, the producer Sam Spiegel and one of the co-stars, Jack Hawkins, with whom Guinness had worked very happily on *The Prisoner*, all began to work on him in earnest, that he finally allowed himself to be convinced.

The rest, as they say, is history. Undoubtedly *Kwai* was the real turning-point in Guinness's career, making him at one fell swoop into an international celebrity rather than merely an actor known internationally by a discriminating minority. From this time on, too, he was quite perceptibly a film star who sometimes appeared on stage rather than a stage actor who sometimes turned an honest penny making films. And at one stroke he had left behind for ever the cosy Ealing-inspired image of the comic grotesque. Though he would appear subsequently in a number of comedies, his Oscar for *The Bridge on the River Kwai* instantly turned him into a plausible dramatic star, and there was no going back: in his one remaining Ealing comedy, *Barnacle Bill*, made the next year, he already seemed too big a gun not to capsize the frail vessel called on to bear it.

No one seems to have foreseen all this at the time. Though the cost of *The Bridge on the River Kwai* escalated alarmingly while the perfectionist Lean was shooting and reshooting and re-reshooting on location in Ceylon, the film was not initially regarded as a blockbuster, and its phenomenal success when released apparently took everyone concerned by happy surprise. Later on Guinness took to saying that Colonel Nicholson was by no means a favourite among his roles, or was even his unfavourite role. No doubt that was the same sort of reaction to excessive fame and obsessive interest that Ingrid

THE BRIDGE ON THE RIVER KWAI
ABOVE: Colonel Nicholson released from solitary confinement.

OPPOSITE, ABOVE: on location with William Holden and Jack Hawkins, AND BELOW: with director David Lean.

Bergman felt when, from encouraging those who had not seen or forgotten *Casablanca* to go and see it, she arrived finally at being so fed up with the subject that she wished heartily people would ask her about something, anything, else. On the other hand, we have no reason to believe that Guinness ever felt very passionately in favour of the role or the film: it was just a job of work, in some ways more interesting, in some ways (especially the arduous locations) more uncomfortable than most. He did, however, contrary to his wont, for once admit when the film was finished that he thought he was 'not bad' in it.

For most others that was the understatement of the century. The role of Nicholson is clearly the dominating one of the film: while the other characters spend most of their footage getting away from the Japanese P.O.W. camp or getting back to it, Nicholson is always there, at the centre of the drama. First, as the senior British officer in the camp, he undergoes solitary confinement and torture when he refuses, on the strength of the Geneva convention, to agree that his officers may work alongside the men on road-building chores, and finally, with great bravery and considerable pig-headedness, wins his point. Then he in a sense reverses his position by taking over the central building enterprise, the construction of the bridge, as his own, a symbol of British discipline and achievement in adversity. He is blinkered, perverse, hopelessly imprisoned in his class and his rank and his military background. He is also, finally, insane, when he has so far lost sight of the war and its real objectives that he resists to the last the strategically necessary blowing-up of the completed bridge. He is a bundle of maddening contradictions, and from most points of view disturbingly inhuman. And yet, as with his cardinal-prisoner a couple of years earlier, Guinness manages to make us see the human being behind the façade most vividly: though Nicholson is in many ways unsympathetic, Guinness makes us care about him without ever sentimentalising things to do it. We know that heroes and saints are the two classes of person we would least care to meet in ordinary everyday life: but Guinness is the actor to convince us otherwise if anyone can.

Recognition of Guinness's individual achievement was generous. He won for his performance the New York Critics' Award, The Golden Globe, the National Board of Review Award, the British Academy Award, the Variety Club Award, and finally, among the seven Oscars won by the film, the coveted American Academy Award for the best male performance of the year. Even his salary was the highest he had earned to date for one film, though considerably less than that of William Holden, who had insisted on a percentage – ten per cent of the film's gross takings, to be paid at $50,000 a year (and even he, astute as he was, did not guess that the film's gross would be so enormous that the studio could pay his annual $50,000 just out of the interest on investing his ten per cent).

The shooting of *Kwai* ran from October 1956 to May 1957. One

ABOVE: Guinness, straight off the set of The Horse's Mouth, *accepts his* Variety Club award for The Bridge on the River Kwai, AND, OPPOSITE, *his Oscar for the same picture.*

suspects that *Barnacle Bill*, made immediately afterwards in time for a Christmas release that year, was deliberately chosen as a way of winding down from the intensities of *Kwai* (and in any case Guinness could not at that point have guessed what an effect the film would have on his life). In the event, *Barnacle Bill* served to demonstrate, if any further demonstration was needed, that the golden days of Ealing comedy were over, and that the famous 'Ealing Spirit' had not survived the dispersal of the physical studio two years earlier, with the consequent drifting apart of the formerly tight-knit team. The group which made Barnacle Bill was still headed by Michael Balcon, and it was scripted and directed by such old faithfuls as T.E.B. Clarke and Charles Frend respectively. But no one's heart seemed to be quite in it. Guinness played cameo roles as six varied but all successfully nautical ancestors of the hero (shades of *Kind Hearts and Coronets*), but most of his time and energies in the film were expended on the title role, that of the hapless descendant hopelessly subject to sea-sickness. The plot involved him in captaining at last a motionless ship – the detached end of a seaside pier – and engaging in a little-man war with

BARNACLE BILL
LEFT: as Bill's Elizabethan explorer ancestor.

OPPOSITE, ABOVE: with Michael Balcon on set (Guinness is made up as another ancestor, an ancient Britain), AND BELOW, at the première.

authority, à la *Passport to Pimlico*. But real comic brio and invention were lacking, and whether anyone knew it or not while the film was in production, it was already too late in Guinness's career (or the history of public taste for that matter) to produce such lame nonsense.

His next film was also a comedy, but of a very different kind. He was still saying that he was not a film star, and alleged in 1957 that his aim in acting was (adapting a phrase of Doctor Johnson's) 'to enable audiences to enjoy life, or the better to endure it'. This being his attitude, it was no doubt not surprising that his eyes should in general be turned towards the comic, even if no longer to comedy of the artless Ealing kind. He was offered the lead in a projected film version of Evelyn Waugh's savage satire on 'the American way of death', *The Loved One*, and was enthusiastic about the idea, though the project for the moment came to nothing. Instead, he determined to take a more decisive part than ever before in the management of his own cinematic destiny by making *The Horse's Mouth*, which he had adapted and scripted himself from Joyce Cary's novel.

Though when faced with a choice he had put aside his writing

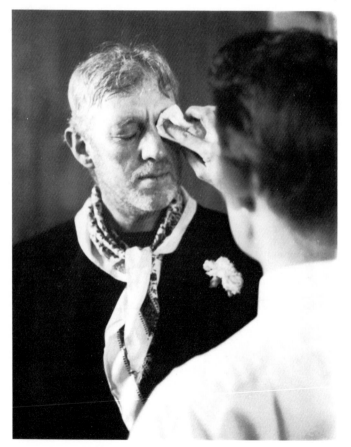

THE HORSE'S MOUTH
LEFT: *being made up for the role of the eccentric painter, Gulley Jimson.*

OPPOSITE, ABOVE, *reflective* AND BELOW, *brain-storming.*

OVERLEAF: *during shooting, in front on one of John Bratby's sketches.*

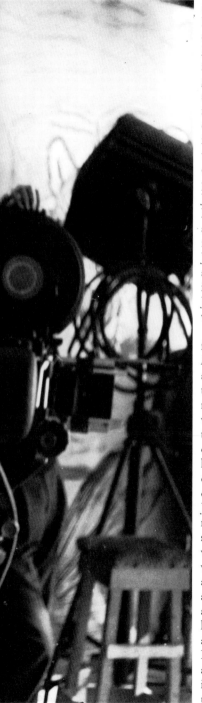

ambitions in favour of acting after the war, the itch to write persisted. His wife encouraged him, especially to beguile the time during an extended theatrical run, and apparently the idea that *The Horse's Mouth* might make a good film was hers. Guinness was reading the novel, and had some difficulty getting through it until Merula's suggestion rekindled his interest: at that point he finished it at a gallop and started at once roughing out a screen treatment. With the enormous success of *The Bridge on the River Kwai* behind him, he was considered a hot property and had little difficulty interesting others in the project as his next starring vehicle. Ronald Neame was engaged to direct and, in an enterprising as well as intelligent move, the most controversial British artist of the moment, John Bratby, was hired to provide the paintings supposed to have been executed by Gully Jimson, Cary's disreputable artist hero. Bratby was at that time the leading figure in the so-called 'kitchen sink' school of British painting, and his strongly coloured, rather expressionistic canvases, based as a rule on scenes of everyday life, provided the perfect counterpart to Jimson's disorderly, obsessive personality and talent. The role was in a way surprising for Guinness to have selected for himself: no doubt it was the extreme change of pace which attracted him, for though Jimson is sly and secretive in certain respects, he is also highly extrovert and a creature of instinct rather than intellect.

If Guinness wanted to show that he could diverge successfully from audience expectations he certainly succeeded with *The Horse's Mouth* – even to the extent that some critics felt his performance was altogether overdone and self-indulgent. Possibly there is a touch of that – there are few films when one feels so strongly that Guinness the man is having a good time indulging Guinness the actor. But it was all worked out with his usual meticulousness. He explained afterwards that he had most trouble deciding on the right voice for the part: he did not want it too rough and working-class, as that did not seem to him correct for projecting Jimson's character. On the other hand, it could not sound in any way prissy or lah-di-dah, as too correct BBC diction would tend to. We are never told in the film exactly where Jimson comes from, but it is easy to presume that he is one of nature's non-conformists, a middle-class drop-out of some kind who has chosen his own eccentric and, in pursuit of his art at least, unscrupulous way of life. Guinness's solution was to roughen the timbre of his voice without suggesting any specific regional or class allegiances: 'It wasn't a question of the grittiness of the voice so much as a question of the accent. Because it seemed to me that it had to be an educated accent and yet if you spoke with an educated accent, a lot of the lines and a lot of situations became not quite believable. If you cockneyed it up a bit it was false to the creation of the book. So it was a compromise. I tried to find a voice in which no one would be able to detect an accent of any sort, a kind of gritty, rough…more or less like air passing out of gravel. And I did find a voice where I thought "I'll have to use that", and it did the trick for me, finding that, because then I felt

113

myself free to relax on that and say the lines and be it.'

The film has very little plot: it is more of a character study in which we see Jimson sometimes very much down on his luck, sometimes unpredictably taken up and with prospects of worldly success which he himself is the first to sabotage. It had a fair if not spectacular commercial success, was in general well-received by the critics, and won Guinness the top acting award at the 1958 Venice Festival (these were the days when British films frequently won acting awards and nothing else at international festivals). More unexpectedly, Guinness's screenplay was nominated for an American Academy Award, which was honour enough even if it did not finally win the Oscar for its category – and especially satisfying for Guinness the part-time writer, who could at least proudly maintain that, little as he had written, it had all been published or performed as intended.

On his next film, *The Scapegoat*, he went even further towards assuming full responsibility for his film-making activities by becoming co-producer of the film with the author of the original book, Daphne Du Maurier. According to Daphne Du Maurier, she had Alec Guinness in mind for the double role at the centre of her story even while writing the novel, and by the time she had completed it was totally convinced that he would be perfect, so sent him the finished result with this suggestion. Guinness was at once fired by the notion of playing a sort of French domestic *Prisoner of Zenda*: he has to be a fairly insufferable French nobleman and the shy Englishman whose identical appearance enables him to be tricked into taking over the count's life for a while. To bring this to the screen Guinness and Du Maurier formed a production partnership, hired Robert Hamer to direct and collaborate on the screenplay with Gore Vidal, signed Bette Davis to co-star as the dowager countess, and Guinness's old ally Irene Worth to play the count's ill-treated wife. On paper, all seemed set fair.

LEFT: *Sheriffs* Punch *cartoon of Eddie Byrne seeing double (or is he?) with two* Guinnesses *in* The Scapegoat.

But anyone who had read the original novel attentively could at once have foreseen the drawbacks. The story is over-complicated and, even given the Englishman's extraordinary command of the French language, quite unbelievable. Nor, having set the situation up, does the author seem to have any clear idea of how to resolve it satisfactorily. One would defy anyone to make a coherent, let alone a compelling, film out of it. Just on the basic script level the obvious problems were never ironed out; Guinness and Bette Davis seem never to have hit it off very well from the start, even though he had chosen her for the role, and Hamer's recurrent drinking problem did not exactly simplify matters. Moreover, when the film was delivered to the distributors, MGM, in rough-cut form, they raised many further objections, the film was radically recut, and in a desperate attempt to salvage something, a voice-over commentary by Guinness was added which was cumbersome as a device and finally explained nothing.

In her memoirs Bette Davis blames Guinness for the debacle: 'When I made *The Scapegoat* with Alec Guinness, he cut my part into such shreds that my appearance in the final product made no sense at

BELOW: family conference from The Scapegoat *with (left to right) Pamela Brown, Noel Howlett, Annabel Bartlett, Geoffrey Keen and Bette Davis.*

all. This is an actor who plays by himself, unto himself, and in this particular picture he plays a dual role, so at least he was able to play with himself.' The judgement is both unfair and acute. Unfair in so far as it seems to blame the post-production vicissitudes of the film on Guinness's artist's ego, when in fact it seems much more likely that his famous lack of self-confidence disarmed him when it came to taking, as producer, a firm line with the distributors who wanted to make idiotic changes. Of all star actors, Guinness would always be the most liable to weakening self-examination and a sneaking belief that his sternest critics were very likely right. On the other hand, in her remarks about Guinness as a loner Bette Davis puts her finger on an important truth. He always stood out in a crowd, or at least stood aside from a crowd, protected by a sort of invisible glass wall from normal human contact. In private life this did not seem to be so: though he fiercely protected his privacy, Guinness was known as a warm and loving friend and family man, a lot of fun at parties and social occasions when he was in the right mood, and, as he said himself, reserved perhaps but not really at all shy. But as an actor he excels in playing characters who are set aside from the rest of humanity by their intellect or their obsessions or their inbuilt inhibitions. Even the apparent extroverts like Gully Jimson or the rollicking Jock Sinclair in *Tunes of Glory* have this sort of apartness at the root of their nature. Many of his characters could, like Soames Forsyte, wish and wish for all the loving in the world: some few have rejected such ideas or just don't care; but whatever their attitude towards loving, one may be sure they don't get it.

In the case of *The Scapegoat* neither Guinness the actor nor Guinness the producer got much loving from anybody, critics, professional associates or the public at large. In the circumstances, one might think it odd that 1959 should have been the year in which Guinness joined the small band of distinguished actors honoured with a knighthood. But thereby hangs a tale. Early in the year, Guinness was asked by the Foreign Office to go as British representative to an international film festival in Mexico City. As it happened, this was a period of particular unpopularity for the British in Latin America, as British policy towards Cuba left something to be desired, and the British Embassy in Mexico was regularly besieged by hostile demonstrators. At the festival, Guinness noticed that all the distinguished foreign visitors spoke in their own languages, with interpreters. So when it was his turn to speak he surprised everybody by delivering a speech in Spanish, which he had learnt by heart for the occasion. At one stroke British popularity was restored in the area, and immediately on his return Guinness was offered the knighthood by Harold Macmillan for the Birthday Honours. A close connection? Who knows? But Guinness has always presumed that there was, and it seems as likely an explanation for the timing of the award as any, even though a knighthood would surely have come Guinness's way sooner or later.

ABOVE: after the knighthood, with wife Merula and son Matthew.

OPPOSITE; TOP: with Fidel Castro while on location for Our Man in Havana, *AND BELOW, with Noël Coward in* Our Man in Havana.

Knighthood or no, the film with which Guinness followed *The Scapegoat* did little better for him, though on paper the prospects seemed impeccable. After all, the two previous collaborations between Carol Reed and Graham Greene, *The Fallen Idol* and *The Third Man*, had been triumphantly successful, and Guinness seemed the very man for the wintry, guilt-ridden world of Greene's best work. True, *Our Man in Havana* was categorised as one of Greene's light-weight (if not altogether light-hearted) 'entertainments' rather than as a serious novel. But still, the central role of Wormold, an unsuccess-ful vacuum-cleaner salesman in pre-Castro Havana who is improbably enlisted by MI5, and keeps his bosses happy with blue-prints of vacuum cleaners until something dangerously like real life catches up with him, would seem to combine enough of Guinness's known qualities, both from Ealing comedy and from more serious work, to make it look like a very suitable vehicle for him. Unfortunately the book itself is again a stumbling-block, being by general consent one of Greene's weakest works – this sort of mild, benevolent satire had never been his forte – and within that the fur-ther problem is that Wormold is hardly characterised at all: he is, as

Guinness put it, 'a blank surrounded by subordinated characters who were more strongly portrayed than he was'. Greene's script does little or nothing to remedy this, and the casting of Noël Coward, Burl Ives and Ernie Kovacs as the more colourful characters impinging, as well as Maureen O'Hara as the main feminine interest, set up a formidable array of not entirely unfair competition. Guinness, as we have seen, was seldom at his best in roles that need to be played largely on strength of personality rather than on inventive craft, and though he decided to play Wormold as 'a much more clearly defined character, an untidy, defeated sort of man,' little of the intention came through in the finished film where, as Noël Coward sadly confided to his diary, 'Guinness is careful, craftsmanlike and rather dull.' In fact, his scenes with Coward are about the liveliest, as the two seem to spark off each other, and in addition the encounter gives rise also to one of Guinness's cleverest imitations, when he is driven briefly by the exigences of the plot to mimic Coward on the phone. But in general the film is disappointingly flaccid and does little for the reputation of any of the distinguished persons concerned.

At least Guinness always after *Great Expectations* had two strings to his bow: if things were not going too well in the theatre he could always shift to films, and if things were not going too well in films he could always turn back to the theatre. That is precisely what he did in 1960, when he was offered the chance to play on stage a role which in the 1930s he had coveted, that of Lawrence of Arabia in Terence Rattigan's play *Ross*. The play had begun life as a film script which was all ready to go into production with Dirk Bogarde in the lead when one of the recurrent economic crises of the British cinema put paid to it. Rattigan then reshaped the material as a stage play, though retaining a quite informal, cinematic structure. Guinness considered himself, at forty-six, too old to play the role on film, but the stage was a different matter, and the part was extensive and varied enough to be an actor's dream, as well as, in its obsessive, interior quality and its apartness from ordinary humanity, being particularly suited to Guinness's own distinctive gifts. It was also very possible for Guinness to find a more immediate sympathy with the character in his vivid, unlocalised sense of his own insufficiency, his desire to escape notice, and in the background (though this does not emerge clearly in the play) his constant, nagging concern over his own illegitimacy.

It is, to say the least of it, curious therefore that Guinness claimed, this time round, to find the character almost entirely antipathetic. In 1939, when playing in *The Ascent of F6*, he had stated that Lawrence was one of his heroes, in that class of adventurers being so far removed from himself that he could not but be drawn. Now, on the contrary, he had come to see the other side of Lawrence, and when talking about him a couple of years later while appearing (not as Lawrence, of course) in *Lawrence of Arabia* he said 'I didn't admire Lawrence. After all, to put the lightest interpretation on it, he was a

OPPOSITE AND BELOW: as T.E. Lawrence in Ross.

ALEC GUINNESS as T. E. LAWRENCE

TUNES OF GLORY

OPPOSITE: Jock Sinclair tries to patch up his affair with a local actress (Kay Walsh).

BELOW: honorary Scots on location – Guinness and John Mills.

fibber. And I find fibbers tiresome.' How are the mightly fallen. However, for the purposes of the play he was able enough to project the heroic side of Lawrence as well as his self-doubts and humiliations. Most spectators felt that this was his finest performance since *The Bridge on the River Kwai*. Noël Coward was in a minority (though a perceptive minority) when he wrote in his diary 'Alec looked very like Lawrence of Arabia and played it well enough, but there was something lacking. He has a certain dullness about him and his "big" moment seemed contrived. He also wore a blond "piece" which was too bright and remained blandly intact even after he had been beaten up and buggered by twelve Turks.' This last observation, incidentally, contains some oblique indication of why the play was so successful: in its frank references to homosexuality it was one of the first in the British theatre to benefit from a new relaxation in the Lord Chamberlain's previous total banning of any direct reference to the subject on stage, and therefore the play seemed a lot more daring and outspoken than it would now appear. But Rattigan's general antiheroic view of Lawrence remains acute, and Guinness captured very well the character as written. That there could be other and more varied dramatic views was to be made clear very shortly in Robert Bolt's script for David Lean's film (1962), but for the moment *Ross* was quite impressive enough, and Guinness not unexpectedly won the *Evening Standard* award that year for his performance in it.

While Guinness was preparing *Ross* he was already putting the finishing touches to a spectacular return to form on screen, though inevitably critics and public knew nothing of it until after his triumph in *Ross* had registered. James Kennaway's novel *Tunes of Glory* has two principal characters, antagonists of almost equal weight: Lieutenant-Colonel Basil Barrow, a rigid disciplinarian and stickler for the rules of military life, and Lieutenant-Colonel Jock Sinclair, the sort of officer who is easy, outgoing and always popular with the men. The first idea of Kennaway and director Ronald Neame was that Guinness should play Barrow, which seemed like obvious type-casting for the man who had played so well that other martinet Colonel Nicholson. Too obvious, thought Guinness, and so he and John Mills, who had originally been thought of for Sinclair, simply swapped roles, to the great delight of both.

Because Sinclair is so popular, so obviously one of the boys, it has been often assumed that he is totally divergent from the usual pattern of Guinness's roles. But when we look more closely, it can be seen that he is no less of a misfit than the rest: his bright and breezy façade hides a hollow man, and one who is no less obsessed and inhuman than his great rival Barrow. Barrow comes, efficient and unlikeable, to take over permanent command of a Scottish army station from Sinclair, who has been in temporary command. The change is not unreasonable or unexpected, nor is it Barrow's fault. But Sinclair resents it and sets out with crazed single-mindedness to undermine Barrow's authority, playing on the easy allegiance of the men to make

121

life unbearable for the newcomer. In the midst of all this plotting he accidentally puts himself in Barrow's power by striking a young corporal in uniform for having formed a romantic attachment with his daughter. Barrow decides to be magnanimous and skip the required court martial if Sinclair will toe the line in future. Sinclair interprets this merely as a sign of weakness, and continues to foment insubordination until finally Barrow kills himself, leaving Sinclair at last abandoned and alone, as much a broken man as he.

Guinness could clearly have been admirable as Barrow. But as Sinclair he completely takes command of the film. The superficial transformation is complete, with a brush of unruly red hair, the easy self-assured grin, the accent perfectly under control: here is the immediate reality of a man who asks himself too few questions until it is too late. But at the same time we can see that Sinclair is a failure as a father, a lover and even as a soldier: for all the man's-man bonhomie, he achieves his popularity too much by currying favour with the men rather than by doing what has to be done and winning their respect. He is isolated without knowing it: though his relations with the soldiers seem to be easy and open, that glass wall is always there. Compared with Barrow, it is the more showy role, but it is also, as is not always the case, the more complex and difficult. Honours were almost equally divided between the two stars, with John Mills this tune carrying off the top acting honours at the Venice Festival where Guinness had triumphed two years before. There was no doubting that, with *Ross* and *Tunes of Glory*, Guinness had returned to full force and vigour in both his favoured areas of activity.

MARKING TIME

After Guinness had played in *Ross* for about the six months, the maximum time he chose to stay put in one role, both he and John Mills departed for America, Mills to play Lawrence in the New York production of *Ross* and Guinness, less wisely, to play a Japanese diplomat in Mervyn LeRoy's Hollywood version of Leonard Spigelgass's Broadway comedy success *A Majority of One*. The role had been played on Broadway by Sir Cedric Hardwicke, who was probably no more convincing as a Japanese than Guinness, except that the eccentric casting could be got away with at a safe theatrical distance, while the close-up scrutiny of the camera was something else again. Nor did the casting of Rosalind Russell as the Jewish widow from Brooklyn who has a holiday affair with Mr Asano exactly help matters, though the film was set up by her husband and she personally intervened to persuade Guinness to accept. Nor did the film's interminable length of 153 minutes for a light comedy (mercifully but still insufficiently pruned by thirty-two minutes for its British showings). Predictably the film got terrible notices, but Guinness was reasonably unaffected: he did it, he said frankly, for the money (£70,000) and even if he was not very good in it, it still ensured that he was immediately offered an endless succession of inscrutable oriental roles by Hollywood producers, in spite of (or perhaps because of) *The Harvard Lampoon's* OK-Doc-Break-the-Arm-Again award for the most extravagant miscasting of the year.

Little more can be said of Guinness's next film, *HMS Defiant* (*Damn the Defiant!* in the States), except that this time he was quite well cast as an humane if somewhat ineffectual commander in the British fleet at the time of the Spithead mutiny, making a suitably sober counterweight to Dirk Bogarde's picturesquely sadistic second-in-command. But it seemed that another role of clinching importance was just round the corner for him: David Lean had what appeared to be a very definite project to film the life of Gandhi for the same production set-up as *The Bridge on the River Kwai*, with Guinness playing the lead. Guinness did a lot of preliminary reading for the role, and Lean even got as far as scouting locations in India, but then the idea was deferred and eventually dropped, not to be taken up again until Richard Attenborough determined to do it and brought it to a triumphant conclusion in 1982. It is one of filmdom's fascinating might-have-beens to consider how Guinness would have tackled the role in the early sixties, and how David Lean, then at the height of his powers, would have directed it.

But Lean was not nonplussed by that particular defeat. He moved on immediately to an alternative notion, that of filming the life of Lawrence of Arabia. No doubt the timeliness of this had had something to do with the success of *Ross* on stage, though the approach of Robert Bolt's screenplay was quite newly thought out. Consistent with Guinness's belief that he was now too old to play Lawrence on screen (he had been worried about this even seven years earlier, when

Previous page: amiably mad in Situation Hopeless – But Not Serious.

Opposite: Japanese diplomat meets Brooklyn widow (Rosalind Russell) in Majority of One.

Opposite: HMS Defiant. *Left: on board with picturesque sadist Dirk Bogarde and assorted mutineers.* *Right: a fond farewell to wife Joy Shelton.*

he was mooted to play the lead in yet another abandoned Lawrence of Arabia project, for Paramount), he was offered instead the key supporting role of Prince Feisal, while the charismatic young Peter O'Toole played the narcissistic and self-deceiving Lawrence. Physically Feisal is one of Guinness's best pieces of disguise: a false nose, slanting eyebrows and a black beard transform him almost out of recognition. But it is his penetration of the mind and personality of the upright but cunning Arab leader which most impresses: the man is in some ways very simple and direct, in others extremely subtle and

LAWRENCE OF ARABIA
OPPOSITE: as Feisal, with Peter O'Toole as Lawrence.

ABOVE: with David Lean on location.

devious. Guinness observed at the time that the longer he played Lawrence on stage, the more fascinated he became with the complex figure of Feisal, and concluded 'Feisal was a gentleman. He had a code which Lawrence lacked.' And therefore must have been far more congenial to the mature Guinness than the show-off Lawrence who had once been one of the young Guinness's idols. Certainly Feisal, though clearly a supporting role, elicits one of Guinness's finest and most memorable screen performances: it is a trait of the true star as well as the actor that he can bring all his talents to bear on a supporting role without overbalancing the film or seeming to bring a sledge-hammer to bear on cracking a peanut.

Feisal, as it turned out, was to be the last first-rate role in a first-rate film that Guinness was to be offered for some time: though he continued activity on all fronts true to his often stated need to be busy (not to mention his other need, which he was never too grand to remind us of, to make a living), the main weight of his activities for the next fifteen years was to be in the theatre. This is not to say that any of his film appearances was totally unworthy, and in several cases more might very reasonably have been expected than actually emerged, for reasons which had nothing to do with Guinness himself. If his film career during these years seemed a bit undirected, that is mainly because the cinema itself was often lacking in a sense of direction, and if Guinness's gifts were not always very well used, that was true of many more actors than him: he was by no means the only person to get lost in all-star mishmashes like *The Fall of the Roman Empire* or to find himself in perfectly respectable films like *Situation Hopeless, But Not Serious,* which were promptly shelved so that almost nobody ever got to see them. But the net result of several such experiences was that when he felt the need of something challenging, something for which he could feel more overall responsibility, he inevitably was now likely to turn to the theatre. And, inevitably as he entered his fifties, he was going to find, like any actor, that opportunities to stretch himself in any medium became rarer: accounting for his generally unfortunate Macbeth in 1966 he said simply that he had grown tired of doing 'lazy work'.

That was the main reason that between *Lawrence of Arabia* in 1962 and *Star Wars* in 1977 he was to star in twelve major theatrical productions and play mainly supporting roles in only eleven films. He inaugurated this new pattern of activity by returning in 1963 to the Edinburgh Festival, where he had not played since his first *Cocktail Party* in 1949, to play the lead in the first English-language production of Ionesco's *Exit the King,* which subsequently transferred to the Royal Court in London for a limited run. He was enthusiastically welcomed back, but in general the play was not well liked, in accordance with a widely held critical view that Ionesco's full-length plays were markedly inferior to his laconic and mysterious one-acters, where his talent was confined to elaborating a single image rather than trying to articulate even a rudimentary plot.

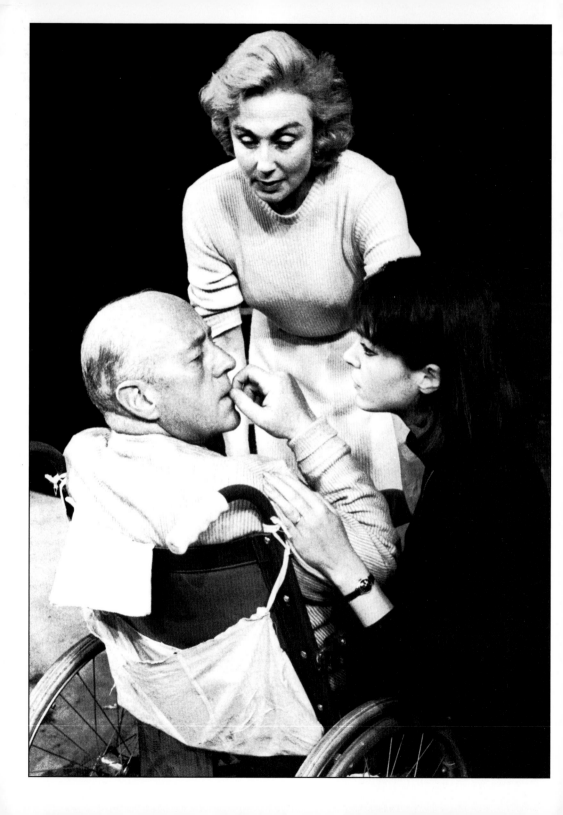

OPPOSITE: *with Googie Withers and Natasha Parry in* Exit the King.

RIGHT: *as Marcus Aurelius in* The Fall of the Roman Empire *with James Mason (left).*

Before going on to his next theatrical endeavour Guinness considered but turned down various film possibilities, including the chance to play one of a pair of aging homosexual kidnappers in an early version of Bryan Forbes's script for his film *Seance on a Wet Afternoon*, and took, somewhat against his better judgement, the role of Marcus Aurelius, Roman philosopher-emperor, in Samuel Bronson's star-studded epic *The Fall of the Roman Empire*. At least the shooting in Madrid afforded him one pleasure: that of getting to know Sophia Loren, who plays his daughter in the film, comparing notes with her on their probable, unwitting encounter in Italy during the war, and being accepted unequivocally by her as having the soul of a Neapolitan. In the film Guinness figures prominently in the first third, before Marcus Aurelius is poisoned in a battle for the succession. He is not in fact called upon to do much but look and act wise, as befits the author of the *Meditations*, and as indeed has always been Guinness's rarest and most evident talent. He also manages to deliver a number of the script's would-be epigrams as though they are a lot wittier than on consideration they prove to be. But his labours, though admirable, are generally lost, and it is understandable that he turned down flat the next offer to be in an all-star costume spectacular, George Stevens's *The Greatest Story Ever Told*.

Again, the theatre rescued him in what one would have said to be his most improbable role ever, as the riotous, hard-drinking Welsh poet Dylan Thomas in Sidney Michaels's play *Dylan* on Broadway. Whose idea that was now appears to be lost in the mists of time, but it can hardly have seemed like obvious casting even at the outset (not like Emlyn Williams playing Thomas in his own biographical compilation) – unless you assume that type-casting for Guinness was to find the character most evidently unlike himself. The result of this apparent mismatching was a grand triumph: Guinness spent six months mesmerising New York audiences, and carried off the Tony Award for that year. When complimented on his performance, Guinness politely demurred: 'Of course, it's not really Dylan Thomas at all that I am playing: just an exaggerated Welsh version of myself if I had tow-coloured hair and drank a lot. I have no reverence for Dylan, or anything like that. He wasn't my kind of person at all. People go on about his voice, but to me it was the voice of a bombastic curate. I really have no interest in the man.' From what we know of Guinness as a person we can well believe this is true. But by what magic, then, does an extraordinarily convincing performance emerge? Naturally the actor does not have to sympathise with the character he plays, or who would play double-dyed villains? But to find somebody presented as a hero antipathetic, or, worse, boring, and yet be able to put him over to an audience? It is all yet another mystery among the many which made up Guinness.

With this success under his belt, Guinness returned to the screen in 1965 in two of what should have been his more compelling films. Alas, it was not to be. *Situation Hopeless, But Not Serious* was based on fellow-actor Robert Shaw's strange first novel *The Hiding Place*, and starred Guinness as a mild-mannered but demented German who keeps two allied servicemen as pets long after the end of the Second World War, playing on their belief that the war is still on and they are surviving only by virtue of his protection. (Eventually they work out the truth, but are so touched by Frick's emotional dependence on them that they take him back to America as a man-servant.) The subject was promising, and Guinness's support from Robert Redford and Michael Connors as the two victims was solid. But Gottfried Reinhardt, who produced and directed, appeared to be fatally undecided about whether he was dealing with an Ealing-type comedy or a kinky psychological drama, and the basic idea was buried under an excessive weight of style. As an eccentric 'little man' Guinness should have been perfectly cast. But perhaps the casting was too perfect and obvious: it could well be that this was just what he meant by 'lazy work', which did not challenge him enough to make him really interested or interesting in the role.

Doctor Zhivago was a disappointment in another way. Not, perhaps, the film as a whole, which was one of the biggest money-makers Guinness had ever been associated with. But his role in it, even though he received top billing, was undistinguished and coincidental: he is really only a narrative device, the half-brother who asks the questions in the framing scenes which enable us to learn the story of Pasternak's doctor-hero in a succession of flashbacks. There was little Guinness could do with the part except to appear neutral and not unsympathetic. Moreover, the film marked a rather decisive break in his professional relationship with David Lean, who, never the warmest and most sympathetic of men with his actors, selected this occasion to cut Guinness down to size by telling him brutally at the outset that he was too old for the part and looked terrible. Guinness was for the moment shattered, but friends advised him to go off and rest for a while and not take Lean's strictures too personally. He followed both pieces of advice, and the shooting itself, in a Madrid covered with fake snow, went off without a hitch. But relations between Guinness and Lean were sufficiently damaged to make it seem very unlikely Guinness would be offered a part in any subsequent Lean film, or if offered would accept. All the same, Guinness remained as ever the perfect gentleman, and after shooting reiterated his belief that Lean was 'easily the most meticulous artist in motion pictures'.

Line-up of principals in Doctor Zhivago; *left to right: Tom Courtenay, Guinness, Geraldine Chaplin, Ralph Richardson, Julie Christie, Omar Sharif, Rod Steiger.*

1966 was Guinness's busiest year for some time: he appeared in two plays on the London stage and made two films in British studios. None of them did much for his reputation, but he could hardly be accused of timidity or of resting on his laurels. The first he did that year was to play Von Berg in Arthur Miller's play *Incident at Vichy*, a close-knit examination of Miller's obsessive themes, loyalty and betrayal, which came to London at just about the lowest point in his critical reputation and was fairly generally dismissed – though a later production of the play benefitted from a revival of his reputation in the later 1970s. Guinness played the one non-Jewish character among the victims of Nazi interrogation, an Austrian prince of unfluffable courtesy and control, who brings a civilised irony to the situation and finally makes the heroic gesture of self-sacrifice without a flicker. If the play excited little favourable attention, Guinness got his least enthusiastic notices in years, being widely accused of walking through the role, or at least of playing it so reticently that he could not avoid charges of dullness and monotony. Uncharacteristically, he observed of this experience: 'Tackling a live audience is like fighting a wild animal.'

The reaction of the critics of *Incident at Vichy* came to look like the acme of enthusiasm when his long-awaited return to Shakespeare occurred later in the year with the opening of his *Macbeth* at the Royal Court. *Macbeth* has the reputation of being an unlucky play, and it is surprising that someone of Guinness's admitted superstitiousness – never whistles in a dressing room and all that – should have undertaken it at all. One of the reasons was apparently that he wanted to work with Simone Signoret, and felt that she had shown in her films the sort of determination and earthy sexuality which would make her, in his view, an ideal Lady Macbeth. Of course, what this left out of account was her ability to manage the English language, not only in a modern colloquial form, but in Shakespearean verse, and to project it well enough on stage, obviously a very different matter from any of her successful English-speaking films. When the production opened, under-rehearsed and plagued by technical mishaps, it was totally damned by the critics. No aspect of direction, design or performance was spared, and Guinness personally got his worst notices since his postwar Hamlet. Again, critics were made uncomfortably aware of the thin line which divides eloquent restraint from plain dullness in Guinness's work: so much depended on the almost silent projection of thought and emotion, with the minimum of external expression, that it was very easy for Guinness to lose that almost telepathic link with the audience on which he importantly depended to communicate. In his Macbeth, as in his Hamlet, conditions were not favourable and it showed. But it also seems possible that he was tempted to the warranted great Shakespeare roles more from a sense of duty than from natural inclination, that he was essentially a modern actor and in the classics that too showed. Certainly on a number of occasions after *Macbeth* he stated clearly that he felt no further temptation to mess with the classics, Shakespearean or otherwise, and though he was briefly interested in the BBC's offer that he should do a *King Lear* for their television Shakespeare series in 1982, his idea of playing Lear as an aging Tolstoi was not thought suitable and the project was, perhaps fortunately, let drop.

Even though *Macbeth* got such a devastating critical reception, it was clear that Guinness's personal popularity had not suffered any: the run at the Royal Court was already completely sold out before the production opened, and played to standing-room only throughout – rather like Peter O'Toole's if anything even more disastrous *Macbeth* at the Old Vic in 1981. Both the films Guinness made in 1966 were very clearly (and not discreditably) aimed at popularity. The film of *Hotel Paradiso*, planned on and off since the stage production of Peter Glenville's adaptation in 1956, finally came to fruition a full decade later, with Glenville again directing and, of course, Guinness starring, along with Gina Lollobrigida, Robert Morley, Peggy Mount, Marie Bell and others almost equally heterogeneous and unlikely. By now it was reasonable to think that Guinness might well be too old for his role of a timid little man trying to carry on a secret romance with his neighbour Lollobrigida, though it would hardly have mattered if the screen treatment had

BELOW AND OPPOSITE: in the controversial Royal Court Macbeth with Simone Signoret as Lady Macbeth.

OPPOSITE: spymaster in The Quiller
Memorandum. *ABOVE: on location
with co-star Robert Helpmann and
director Guy Hamilton.*

been more sprightly. But Peter Glenville's touch seemed a lot heavier
on film than in the theatre, Feydeau's clockwork plotting tended to go
awry on the wide-screen, away from the rigid conventions of the
stage, and the cast never came near to subduing their various styles
and mannerisms to one coherent approach. The film was another, like
Situation Hopeless, which played a few previews then was quickly
shelved and vanished from view for years or for ever, unseen even by
the most enthusiastic Guinness fans except, perhaps, finally on some
television late-late show.

   The Quiller Memorandum had a far more honourable career.
Scripted by Harold Pinter from the novel by Adam Hall (Elleston
Trevor), it was an efficient incursion into the currently fashionable
spy and counter-spy genre, which was simultaneously being played
for laughs and thrills in the James Bond cycle or being given the
resolutely downbeat John Le Carré treatment in *The Spy Who Came
in from the Cold. The Quiller Memorandum* was betwixt and between:
a moderately serious tale of a spy (Quiller – played by George Segal)
at grips with a sinister neo-Nazi organization headed by Max von
Sydow. Guinness got second billing as Quiller's smooth old-school-
tie chief, and was coolly efficient in a way which, nowadays, suggests
to us his future ability to play le Carré's spy-master Smiley. But
here he did not have much more to do than register a fairly conventional character's few distinguishing features and nip out
again sharpish.

   Of his two major acting jobs in 1967 it was again, predictably, the theatrical one which offered the bigger challenge, but the cinematic one actually showed Guinness's talents to better advantage. And since neither was notably successful it did not make very much difference either way. Simon Gray's *Wise Child*, which Guinness played at Wyndham's Theatre, is a vaguely sub-Orton piece which exploits a mildly outrageous idea for rather more than it is worth. Guinness played in it an apparently blowsy middle-aged woman travelling with her son round a faded south coast boarding house circuit such as he must have known all too well from his own peripatetic childhood. Fairly soon it transpires that 'Mrs Artminster' is in fact Jack Masters, the Peabody Postman's assailant, and is in drag, on the run from the police. The game is nearly given away when 'she' makes a pass at the black maid, but smoothed over until a getaway can be arranged, leaving the 'son' to the tender mercies of the homosexual landlord. Guinness seemed to have fun with the disguise, but there was not enough character there for him to get his teeth into, and the performance, like the play, soon slipped from memory.

WISE CHILD

*'Mrs Artminster' seems quite comfortable (*OPPOSITE*) until she starts to get a bit too friendly with the hired help, Cleo Sylvestre (*BELOW*).*

THE COMEDIANS

OPPOSITE: Major Jones has to don some odd disguises.

BELOW: In conference with Richard Burton, James Earl Jones, Elizabeth Taylor and Peter Ustinov.

The Comedians continued Guinness's association with Peter Glenville and was also for Guinness a return to Graham Greene. On neither count was the repeat too happy: the story, as adapted from his novel by Greene himself, was rambling and unfocused, and Glenville did not succeed in pulling this project together either. The main purpose of the novel was an attack on the dictator of Haiti, 'Papa Doc' Duvalier, and his rule, but the film lost this from view, wasting far too much time exploring the not very interesting love affair of a local hotel owner (Richard Burton) and the German wife (Elizabeth Taylor) of an ambassador (Peter Ustinov). Also around in subsidiary plots are Paul Ford and Lillian Gish. Guinness is at least central to the real subject as a phony British major who is imprisoned, escapes, and is killed trying to help the freedom fighters. Guinness clearly relished the charming, disreputable Major Jones, spinner of tall stories whose cheek and bluff have never managed to carry him quite far enough in life. It is a subtle, inventive performance, which even allows him a few more moments in drag as a swivel-hipped cook in blackface. But the film as a whole was such a damp squib he might as well not have been in it for all the good it did him.

Though Guinness had on occasion said that he would never appear on stage again, no one took him very seriously, and probably he did not himself really believe it. In 1968 he retreated once more to the stage, reviving his old role of Sir Henry Harcourt-Reilly in a new production of *The Cocktail Party*, first at the Chichester Festival and then transferred to London. It was a safe move, but also a wise one: his reading of the role had deepened through the years, and also got superficially stronger. The elfin, faintly sinister elements in the character were still present, emphasised it anything by the beard he wore this time to underline a fleeting resemblance to Sigmund Freud. This was a substantial success for him, but it seemed to be also a sign that he was slowing down: it was all he did in 1968, and he did nothing new in 1969.

The Cocktail Party, *with and without beard.* LEFT: *in London with Eileen Atkins;* OPPOSITE, *in Chichester.*

In 1970 he played on stage in *Time Out of Mind* at the Yvonne Arnaud Theatre, Guildford; the production did not, as expected, come into London, very likely because of the ingrained oddity of the whole project. It was a new play by Bridget Boland, with whom Guinness had worked so successfully on *The Prisoner*, and the subject had faint but unmistakable overtones of *The Man in the White Suit*: eccentric idealist in an industrial laboratory pitted against the forces of big business. However, this was an idealist with a difference: it gradually emerges that his wisdom and wide-ranging knowledge – he seems absurdly over-qualified for a humble laboratory assistant – come from his being six hundred years old, a medieval alchemist whose quest for the elixir of life was rewarded, so that he has turned into a kind of Tithonus-cum-Wandering Jew, seeking death but unable to achieve it. The point of placing him in a modern context, of course, is to give an ironic (or tragic) new perspective on the follies of modern science and mankind's headlong rush to nuclear disaster. But to do this the play required us to accept fiendish caricatures for the forces of modern industry, and stretched credulity to breaking point in depicting the motiveless malevolence of all and sundry towards the saintly hero. For Guinness it was another exercise in the elfin and elusive: *The Times* aptly described his performance as 'seraphic'. He even got to do one of his little dances à la *The Cocktail Party* to illustrate the music of the spheres. But on consideration this did not look like very convincing West End fare.

Also in 1970 Guinness played Malvolio with distinction (Ralph Richardson again playing Sir Toby Belch), in a television production of *Twelfth Night* he later described brusquely as 'dull', and made two films, *Cromwell* and *Scrooge*. *Scrooge*, directed by his old friend and collaborator Ronald Neame, was a cheery musical version of *A Christmas Carol*, modelled rather after *Oliver!*, and in it Guinness played, with the greatest possible relish, Marley's Ghost, funny and extravagant and sinister all at once. While doing so he suffered a painful hernia, which did not make life any easier for him in the next year or two. In *Cromwell* he played Charles I, making an attractive and courageous figure out of the principal antagonist to Richard Harris's heroic *Cromwell*. Their performances were well matched, but the film was in general rather stolid and old-fashioned, and again it was the theatre which prevented Guinness from falling into conventional doldrums.

The occasion this time was John Mortimer's autobiographical play *Voyage Round My Father* at the Haymarket. Here there were human and technical challenges aplenty. To begin with, the piece is a reasonably loving account of a monster, and the actor playing the father has somehow to indicate the love as well as the monstrosity. Also, the father is blind, and the actor has to find a way of indicating that without running the risk, as Guinness put it, of 'spending the whole evening being so clinically blind that you don't get on with the acting of it, so to speak.' In the event, after experimenting

Opposite: in Time out of Mind *at Guildford.*

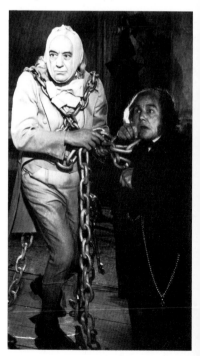

Below: Marley's ghost intimidates Scrooge (Albert Finney).

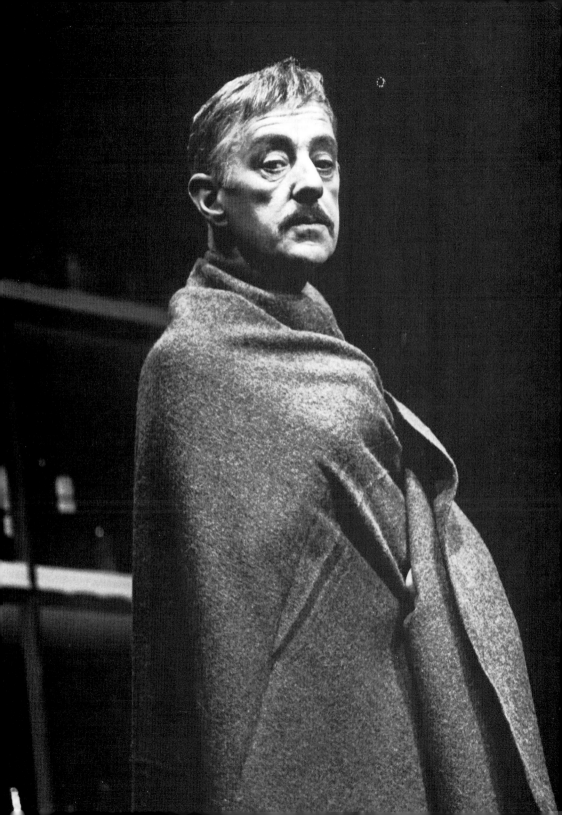

CROMWELL

ABOVE: Punch *caricature of Guinness as Charles I.*

ABOVE LEFT: between takes, in discussion with director Ken Hughes.

BELOW LEFT: Charles comforts his children.

With Nicola Pagett in A Voyage Round My Father.

with keeping the eyes totally closed, which rather fazed his fellow actors, and keeping them always half-open, which tended to confuse him, he worked out a sort of time chart of where they should be closed and where he could afford for them to be open. Presumably members of the audience further back than the first three rows could scarcely be conscious of that anyway, but for Guinness the technical aspects had to be all neat and tidy before the feeling could begin to be right.

Lovable as well as monstrous Guinness undoubtedly was – more so, surely, than Laurence Olivier when he played the same role a decade later on television. It was one of Guinness's more distinctive features that he did not need, emotionally and for his own well-being, to be playing a 'nice man'. He could play, as we have seen, with full actor's empathy, a role with which he had no personal sympathy at all. And he was aloof enough not to need us to sympathise either. This is precisely what made him so admirable in a role like that of Mortimer père: he never by a flicker appealed for our sympathy or even pity, played no actor's tricks to make us love him in spite of all evidence that we should do the contrary. Whatever liking for, or, perhaps more important, understanding of the character that we might achieve was absolutely inherent, bathed in the cold clear light of Guinness's own critical intelligence.

All this is very important in relation to his most important film role in 1973, that of Hitler in *Hitler – The Last Ten Days*. How, after all, could any actor be likely to feel much warm, human sympathy with anyone quite so monstrous? And yet an all-out onslaught would be self-defeating. Even as it was, Guinness's Führer at his last gasp was felt to be too comfortable, even too human to carry total conviction, and the film, made in a mere eight weeks by an Italian company, was another which vanished from circulation very rapidly and was seen by few. Guinness's comments on his preparation for the role are, however, significant: 'I suppose the only attitude I have is one of reasonable objectivity – at least as objective as one can get when playing such a man. You might say I play him with a touch of irony, but certainly not with any deliberate emphasis. I do know that Hitler will not be caricatured in this picture. There is nothing funny about him. In the first shots I don't have the lock across the forehead. I don't want the audience to start by saying "There he is, old Hitler". I am going to try and be objective in creating the man he was at the time.' While Hitler was unmistakably the extreme instance, Guinness might have said much the same for every role he ever played.

OPPOSITE: as the Pope in Brother Sun, Sister Moon.

LEFT: made up for the title role in Hitler – The Last Ten Days.

Around this time Guinness felt himself unable to play the role of Wagner in Visconti's *Ludwig*, which he had at first tentatively accepted, and it was played, more suitably perhaps, by Trevor Howard. When Laurence Olivier backed out of playing the small but important part of the worldly Pope in Zeffirelli's St Francis film *Brother Sun, Sister Moon*, however, Guinness agreed to take over. He comes in only right at the end of the film, when Francis, denounced by conservative elements in the church for his informality and lack of ceremony, appeals to the Pope and finally receives papal approval for his apostolate to the poor and the simple. Guinness, immensely bearded and wrinkled and bagged, made a profound impression with his very brief footage in this inordinately pretty film.

Also in 1973 he began another fruitful collaboration, with the playwright Alan Bennett, by appearing in his play *Habeas Corpus*, and turned for the first time significantly to television. Up to now he had been rather hesitant about the small screen. Back in 1959 he had done a play called *The Wicked Scheme of Jebal Deeks*, a variation on *The Man in a White Suit* idea, for American television, and had done some fancy side-stepping since to avoid further involvement – even when it

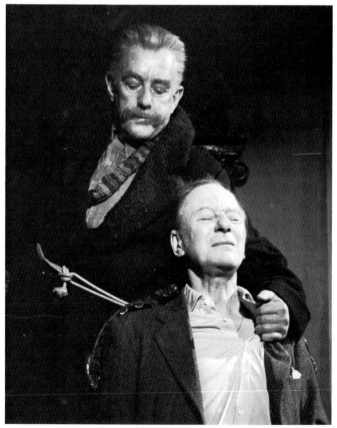

Executioner and victim, Guinness and Gielgud in Conversation at Night.

might have been as profitable as a million-dollar offer in 1960 to produce and appear in a dozen beer commercials.

In 1969 he had been tempted by the chance of working with John Gielgud again, after many years – more, no doubt, than either of them cared to remember – in a thirty-minute Dürrenmatt duologue, *Conversation at Night*, in which he played a political executioner and Gielgud the victim. The ATV *Twelfth Night* he preferred to forget. But now he agreed to star in a major new television play by John Osborne, *The Gift of Friendship*, a wayward piece about a famous author of eccentric and combative disposition (supposedly based on Evelyn Waugh) and followed it with a lush production of Shaw's *Caesar and Cleopatra*, in which he made a delightful feline and whimsical ruler of the world opposite Genevieve Bujold's kittenish queen of Egypt. (His view of Shaw: 'I really think that any fool could play Shaw, provided he can be heard and seen and is able to stand still.')

When Laurence Olivier first appeared in a John Osborne play or, much later, when John Gielgud first appeared in a Pinter, there was a newsworthy sense of the unexpected, of two different worlds coming together. For all the other things these actors had done in their lives, they were overwhelmingly associated in the public mind with the classics, the theatrical Establishment, and the 'New Drama' was decidedly anti-establishment, a challenge to all that they were supposed to stand for. It is a clear indication of Guinness's apartness among the theatrical knights that no one was at all surprised when he was in a new Osborne play or a play by an even younger dramatist like Alan Bennett. He had always been a modern actor, and there was no essential distinction between playing Clemence Dane in the thirties or Rattigan and Eliot in the forties and playing Osborne and Bennett in the seventies. In any case neither new play was exactly what one would call experimental.

Habeas Corpus is in fact almost a farce, though not quite – Bennett noted at the time that he had removed the word 'farce' from the text in a couple of places, so as not to mislead his audience. It is rather an atmospheric, reflective piece which uses a lot of the machinery of farce – amatory intrigue, mistaken identity, the awkward loss of vital clothing at crucial moments – for quite non-farcical ends: the play can even be read as a meditation on death. Guinness's role was an intriguing one for him: superficially he was required to radiate his usual philosophical calm as a Hove general practitioner centrally embroiled in the comic intrigue, but having established this persona at the outset he then had constantly to undercut it by revealing himself as, beneath the sanctimonious surface, a sly lecher with a burgeoning and thoroughly disreputable fantasy life. His comic timing was, as ever, immaculate, and his ability to sketch in incongruities with the utmost economy, a nod or a wink or an unguarded gesture, kept audiences happy in his most clear-cut stage success for some years.

Family groups from Habeas Corpus, ABOVE: *(left to right) with Phyllida Law, Guinness, Margaret Courtenay, Christopher Good and Patricia Hayes.* LEFT: *Hewison's* Punch *cartoon.*

As the 1970s progressed it certainly seemed as though Guinness was slowing up, taking things easier. For some reason interviewers kept asking him whether he was rich; they never seemed so crass as to ask the other knights directly, but perhaps film stars as apart from theatrical luminaries were supposed to be rich and ready to tell everyone. Guinness always replied politely that he was not rich, was not even financially secure. Though he had made very decent amounts of money, there were also thin years – he claimed to have made only £90 in 1970, though he was not at all sure why. So he had to go on working to make a living, as well as from the professional satisfactions he derived from acting and his own personal need to be busy. But as he entered his sixties there did not seem to be the need to do so much, and he was growing wary of the kind of insecurity which had in the past driven him to do everything he was asked to do, on the assumption that he might never be asked again, or at least on a feeling of 'Well, I don't know, it isn't terribly good, but the next one might be even worse, so I'd better do this'. A few years earlier he had confessed 'I'm insecure, like most actors. Of course one learns to live with it, after a fashion. Each morning it's simply a question of *How insecure shall I feel today?* One never knows, does one?' The basic feeling might not have changed much, but what good is maturity if it does not bring a certain tranquillity?

This being his present situation, he was more inclined to pick and choose his roles. In 1975 he appeared only on stage, in Julian Mitchell's adaptation of Ivy Compton Burnett's idiosyncratic novel about the horrors of family life *A Family and a Fortune*. The very formal dialogue of this author takes surprisingly well to the stage, and Guinness made the most of its elegant ironies, though in other respects it was a very uncomfortable experience, as the cast toiled through one of the hottest summers on record, in an un-airconditioned theatre (the Apollo), wearing heavy Edwardian clothes, while members of the audience were regularly carried off, night after night, fainting from the heat. In 1976 he made one of his rare visits to Hollywood, to play the blind butler Bensonmum in Neil Simon's elaborate burlesque of classic detective fiction *Murder by Death*. It was another all-star extravaganza, bringing together parody versions of the Thin Man and his wife, Charlie Chan, Sam Spade and Hercule Poirot in a competition to solve a murder, and it is as likely the butler did it as anyone else. Or as unlikely, for the film is much too broadly relishing of its own jokes to command even our most superficial, conditional involvement in trying to work out the solution to the conundrums it proposes. In any case, Guinness's part, small to begin with, ended up largely on the cutting-room floor, leaving only a few glimpses, all played on the same level of knockabout farce as the rest of the film. However, Guinness made no excuses: 'It was a very funny film,' he said. 'The script made me laugh – and not many things in recent times have done that.' Though he did add 'It's a little bit wordy' – which was putting it mildly.

OPPOSITE: in Hollywood, on the set of Murder by Death *with David Niven.*

BELOW: making himself up as Dean Swift for his own play Yahoo.

Things were, in any case, bowling along quite nicely, and Guinness's mind was full of a new personal venture, appearing on stage in a new play of his own, *Yahoo*, based on the life and writings of Johnathan Swift. At least, it was not exactly a play, but not, either 'one of those readings against black velvet curtains.' And for once, unlike his very guarded-to-hostile responses to the other real-life characters he had played, his response to Swift was totally enthusiastic: 'I'm mad about him'. He described the origin of the piece: 'The idea came out of a charity programme I did at Aldeburgh and somewhere else – I've forgotten where. I'd concocted a thing about London and the people who had lived in London and in it I read a page from the *Journal to Stella* in which Swift described taking a swim at Chelsea. It struck me on both occasions when I read it that it went

THE SUNDAY TIMES, OCTOBER 3 1976

37

Frank Herrmann

down better than anything else, and I began to wonder if he speaks to the modern world? I thought I'd have a shot at putting together some of his work. I did some extensive research and got half the programme together and then found myself really stymied. At that point I had to go off to Hollywood so I asked Alan Strachan, who had directed *A Family and a Fortune*, who is a good scholar, whether he would like to come in with me on it. When I came back from Hollywood we spent three or four weeks on it and got a shape together. We saw eye to eye on most things.'

It must seem, on the face of it, curious that the mild-mannered and reticent Guinness should be drawn so strongly to the savage Dean. But clearly he found in Swift's writings an echo of his own interests, his own angers, and Swift's 'marvellous freedom from cant and contempt for politicians' were certainly sympathetic qualities. Even though Guinness accepted that Swift treated the women in his life abominably, he was inclined to make allowances in Swift's case that he could not for T.E. Lawrence or Dylan Thomas. Yet another mystery among the many Guinness mysteries. But there was no doubt that *Yahoo* was a labour of love. Before it opened Guinness discounted the possibility of its being a commercial success, but hoped it might have a little run so that it would have a chance to make its point. When it was suggested to him that his presence in the cast was bound to ensure that he quickly denied it: 'Oh no, no one has that power, except possibly Gielgud and Richardson.' But of course he was wrong: in the West End of the mid-Seventies there were few safer draws than Guinness, and insecurities or no, he had little reason to doubt it.

During the summer while he was planning *Yahoo* he agreed to make, almost accidentally and without too much thought, an appearance in an unpretentious science fiction film – just because he found the script unexpectedly gripping to read. It is doubtful if he or anyone else had the slightest inkling of the difference this decision was going to make in his career. For who would expect anything much of a film called *Star Wars*...?

INDIAN SUMMER

No one would maintain that Obi-Ben Kenobi is Guinness's finest performance or represents the peak of his acting career. And yet it would not be wise to underestimate the ability to carry off such a role in such a context. To say nothing of the transformative effect the almost inconceivable success of *Star Wars* had on Guinness's standing with the public and perhaps even with himself. For one thing, being associated, in whatever capacity, with one of the most enormously money-making films in the history of the cinema is not to be sneezed at especially when, like Guinness's, one's pay includes two and a half per cent of the gross take – though before anybody could get too excited at the idea of two and a half per cent of some $200 million, Guinness quickly pointed out just how much of that goes to the tax man. Even so, it must have meant that Guinness needed never to work again and was at last financially secure, which must have made a difference to the life, if not necessarily the life-style, of a man so wedded to insecurity. The one thing it evidently did not mean is that he would never work again: he soon amply demonstrated that. But at least he would work because he wanted to, on things he wanted to do, rather than to keep the wolf from the door.

But all this is to anticipate. When, on the last day's shooting on *Murder by Death*, Guinness was sent a script by a young Hollywood film-maker whose very name was unfamiliar to him, he had no reason to expect any such spectacular results. But he found himself reading this inter-galactic fairy story with enough interest to go to the trouble of checking up on Lucas's previous work, and went to see his earlier hit *American Graffiti*. He was suitably impressed by the directness, the natural sentiment and the story-telling skill of that, and so decided to do *Star Wars*, though even after the end of the shooting (on location in Tunisia as well as in a hot studio during a hot summer) he was heard to observe 'I don't know who I was playing.' He was particularly impressed by George Lucas personally, his quietness and control: 'Like all the best directors Lucas had very little to say during the actual filming. He simply sensed when you were uncomfortable and just walked across and dropped a brief word in your ear. It was almost like being on stage: good actors don't like being told how to act and they become worried if they are made to feel merely part of someone else's work…In this total concentration, in his reliance on both his eye and his ear, he reminded me of the young David Lean. I always had the feeling that, like Lean, deep down he was totally involved in the action. Of course there was none of the Lean star-quality, the hush when The Director Is On Set. But there is the sensation that life can only be a piece of celluloid. Lucas is completely wrapped up in the cinema, he is only happy talking film. Lean is a bit like that, too, but he is interested in horticulture, ornithology and listening to Beethoven's Seventh as well…'

And despite alleged mystification over the character he was playing (and some reservations about the quality of the film's dialogue) Guinness never had any doubt about the value of the fairy-story

PREVIOUS PAGE: The improbable star – as George Smiley in Smiley's People.

OPPOSITE: intergalactic wise man – Obi-Ben Kenobi in Star Wars.

OVERLEAF, TOP LEFT: on location for Star Wars *with director George Lucas. BOTTOM, LEFT: leading Luke Skywalker (Mark Hamill) through the labyrinth. RIGHT: the climactic duel.*

per se. He felt that the film had not so much a message for our own specific time – as others optimistically insisted when 'The Force be with you' became a catch-phrase – but a general appeal to children of all ages who wanted their goods to be good and their bads to be unspeakably horrid and everything to work out all right in the end. As for his own part in it, as the last of the Jedi Knights, guardians of truth and wisdom in a universe increasingly dominated by the dark and evil Empire, its general purpose and significance were clear enough. Even, possibly, too clear for an actor to feel he could make much of the role. But here if anywhere Guinness's quality as a star as well as a character actor comes out: he not so much plays as *is* Obi Ben Kenobi. Even if his qualities of conveying thought on screen, of suggesting deep seriousness and idealism without seeming inhuman, were not explored in depth by the role, the unmistakable fact of his presence fleshed out the role and gave it a simple power – force as well as Force – which hardly any other actor could have brought to it.

And this sheer star-power told: despite a bevy of attractive young people in the leading roles, Guinness was the only human being (well, sort of) in the film who could stand up to the charms of its two robots, C-3P0 and R2-D2, the happiest comedy combination since Laurel and Hardy. He virtually stole the film, and clearly deserved every penny of his astronomical remuneration, however much or little of it he actually received. And suddenly he was one of the cinema's hottest properties again – hotter perhaps than ever before. Typically, the first thing he did after the success of *Star Wars* became assured was to change direction again, and go straight back to the theatre. What tempted him was a new play by Alan Bennett.

The Old Country is again, like *Habeas Corpus*, an atmospheric comedy with a more serious point than at first meets the eye. Technically it resembles more a whodunit than a farce this time: holding its cards very close to its chest, it only very gradually reveals that the principal characters, overwhelmingly English and conservative as they are, are living not in a stockbroker-belt cottage, but a dacha in Russia, where they have become political exiles. For Guinness is a senior member of the Foreign Office who defected, but remains absurdly attached to 'the old country', seen and conformed to as some sort of Ealing comedy abstraction of humanity and gentility rather than as something real, growing and changing. It is a role rich in irony – some of it in the minds of the audience, observing the character, but a lot of it, finally, within the character himself, someone much more formidable than he first appears, a modest snob who can in extremes rap out a savage insult or even resort to his revolver. Guinness predictably had a field-day with the role, which might have been – and quite possibly was – made to measure for him.

Having thus triumphed successively in the cinema and the theatre, he proceeded to turn himself into a triple threat by doing, for the first time, something he had sworn he would never do: starring in a television serial. The temptation, of course, was exceptional. Guinness

Opposite: as Hilary, the political exile in The Old Country.

had for some time admired the works of John Le Carré, with their bleak and wintry world not so far removed from that of another favourite author, Graham Greene. So when he was approached by a group working on a seven-part television adaptation of Le Carré's *Tinker, Tailor, Soldier, Spy*, including Le Carré himself (or David Cornwell, to use his real name), he paid more than his usual attention to such offers, met producer, director, adaptor and author at L'Etoile for lunch, got on very well with them, and decided to take the plunge. The role he was offered was, needless to say, that of Le Carré's spymaster, George Smiley.

As George Smiley in Tinker, Tailor, Soldier, Spy *and* Smiley's People. LEFT: *on Horse Guards Parade.* OPPOSITE, TOP: *with Patrick Stewart;* BELOW: *on location with Sian Phillips.*

OVERLEAF: *Smiley at work in* Smiley's People.

The Le Carré serial was going to take six months out of Guinness's life, so he decided to do it all properly, even going out of his way, at Le Carré's suggestion, to meet the alleged 'original' of Smiley, former head of MI6, Maurice Oldfield. Oldfield was very friendly, and evidently knew just what was up: after the series aired he wrote Guinness a note saying 'I still can't recognise myself'. And in fact it was unlikely that Guinness would get material for mimicry from the meeting – that was never his way, and it was more a general feeling of the character and his world that could be useful to the actor. Guinness was very conscious that he did not look as Smiley was described in the book: he felt he should have been seven years younger, a stone heavier and two or three inches shorter. All of which is true, except that anyone who has ever read the books now sees Smiley as Guinness, so close was the identification between actor and role.

For Guinness the keynote of Smiley's character was his vulnerability. He is depicted as immensely intelligent, guarded, authoritative, and yet with an Achilles heel in matters of personal emotion, particularly where they concern his beautiful, unfaithful wife. The main problem in playing the role was to convey the vulnerability without making viewers wonder how someone so vulnerable could wield such power, and to convince that the character is intelligent without, often, much dialogue to do so: 'If you have someone like Smiley who's meant to be tremendously intellectual and hugely bright, obviously he's going to be silent much of the time precisely when he's listening to people and working things out. Well, you can't flick your eyes around as if to say "I'm being bright." It's got to be played exactly the opposite, blank, or so it seems to me, or that's how it came out. So there are, I should think, innumerable close-ups of me just looking bored, which are just when one's got to persuade the audience one's taking in everything that is being said.'

Though Guinness, after completing work on *Tinker, Tailor, Soldier, Spy*, was plagued by his usual self-doubts ('I've probably gone overboard...People may say I haven't acted it anyway. I always feel I've made a mess of it. I probably have'), when the series finally went on the air in September 1979 it was immediately judged a triumph, one of the best things in British television, and certainly an enormous personal success for Guinness. With *Star Wars*, *The Old Country* and *Tinker, Tailor, Soldier, Spy* under his belt in just three years, he could surely do anything he wanted – or, if he wanted, nothing ever again.

But the itch to work could not be stilled. If asked why his failure rate was lower than that of any of the other actor-knights, he would reply 'I can only conclude that they are like I was when younger, thinking this is the last chance I have of making a few thousand pounds. I cannot believe that they have done some of the things for sheer pressure for money. It can come out of a humility in a way. Or it is people who talk you into things, so often.'

No one, anyway, was now going to talk him into anything he did not want to do, one way or another. Perhaps it might be out of per-

ABOVE: survivor in Raise the Titanic.

sonal loyalty, as in the case of the two follow-ups to *Star Wars*, *The Empire Strikes Back* (1980) and *Return of the Jedi* (1983), in both of which, though he had originally feared their advent, he made token appearances to round off the story. Obviously no one but he could play Smiley in the second series from the same team, *Smiley's People* (1982), and no one did, though he firmly added 'There won't be a third series. Or if there is, I won't be in it.' It was not too clear what he was doing, for any reason, in an all-star disaster movie (or disaster of a movie) *Raise the Titanic*, playing, briefly, a frail but determined survivor. But he obviously enjoyed playing Freud for laughs (having so often played him indirectly, as in his last *Cocktail Party*) in the Dudley Moore film *Lovesick*, even if the film was no great shakes. Equally, he seemed to revel in guying himself in the 1980 *Morecambe and Wise Christmas Show*: one recalls that an earlier guest of the couple, Glenda Jackson, observed that their direction was very simple – 'Faster, louder!' – and when asked if that was good advice replied 'The best'.

Above all, any suspicion that he might be appearing in Jack Gold's remake of that famous old weepie *Little Lord Fauntleroy* (for televi-

OPPOSITE: as Freud in Lovesick.

sion in the States and theatrical showing elsewhere) just for the money was very rapidly dispelled, both by his crisp, unsentimental performance as Little Lord Fauntleroy's craggy, unforgiving but finally softened guardian and by his remarks on reading the script: 'I thought, this is very gutsy, this isn't sloppy, and why do I keep bursting into tears? And one realised of course that it's the great adjectival passages – the golden hair and all that – which make it seem, you know, well, all sloppy. I was very impressed, it was great fun to do, and I haven't seen one frame of it.' But he liked the idea well enough to break another rule and actually attend the film's Royal premiere for the benefit of the Red Cross. After all, if one is a star, one must eventually do the occasional star-like thing…

But the most interesting enterprise of all was undoubtedly *A Passage to India*. In 1983 it was thirteen years since David Lean had made a film, and eighteen since he and Guinness had had their falling out over *Dr Zhivago*. Lean was seventy-five, and it seemed unlikely that, rich, famous and loaded with honours as he was, he would ever make a film again. But then, suddenly, it was announced that he was to go ahead with a project he had long cherished – at least since his trips to India in 1962 preparing the abortive Gandhi film which was to star Guinness. *A Passage to India*, based on E. M. Forster's novel, was to go into production on Indian locations in November. And what more appropriate that, any lingering discomfort in the relationship long forgotten, he should ask Guinness to play the role of Professor Godbole, the tranquil, philosophical Hindu, and that Guinness should agree? It was like the closing of a circle: those who were first united in Guinness's first film were coming together yet again for, as it proved, a final consecration of Lean's talent – though not, perhaps, of Guinness's, since he never seems totally happy in the role, and several key scenes, such as one in which he did yet another of his enigmatic little dances, were removed in the editing.

Before the film opened to a triumphant response in the United States towards the end of the year, Guinness had already, if not closed another circle, at least returned again to a problem which had clearly been long niggling at him: the problem of Shakespeare. This time it was through the chance to play Shylock in a new production of *The Merchant of Venice* as part of the summer season at Chichester Festival Theatre. A new generation of critics, who for the most part hardly remembered his difficulties with Macbeth eighteen years before, were inclined to be enthusiastic about his played-down, very human interpretation of the part, especially in the context of a determinedly anti-revisionist, Jewish-villain interpretation in Stratford shortly before. But the rest of the production and most of the supporting cast came in for hard knocks, and it was decided not to transfer the production to London once the season was over, so the latest Guinness/Shakespeare confrontation remained finally unresolved, though it appeared that Guinness might at last be winning out.

In his spare time (what spare time?) Guinness had been working on a book which he said, with characteristic nicety (or, as some might think, characteristic perversity), 'my publishers, though not of course I, regard as an autobiography'. When *Blessings in Disguise* came out in 1985, both proved to be right, It is probably the only sort of auto-biography Guinness, with his famous dislike of the first person, could ever write. He appears in it largely as a peripheral figure, the observer of and reactor to a variety of people he has known. Nor, of course, is this elegantly written book an exercise in name-dropping. Though some of the pen portraits are of famous people like the Sitwells, particularly Edith, Guinness is also eager to give full weight to more obscure or unfairly forgotten people who have influenced him or whom he admired, such as his old teacher Martita Hunt and the eccentric actor Ernest Milton. He does, incidentally and almost apologetically, tell us more than ever before about his chequered childhood and his attempts to solve the mystery of his father's identity – from which latter, though the most likely candidate seems to be Andrew Geddes, the only sensible verdict remains 'not (quite) proven'.

BELOW: Playing Professor Godbole in David Lean's epic, A Passage to India.

His next screen appearance, as the eponymous hero of Graham Greene's *Monsignor Quixote* in a television film of the book, was pleasant enough, but for him rather too undemanding casting: he slips so easily into Greene's world that it can all be done on automatic, with a twinkle here and a touch of inscrutability there, and disappointingly little to retain the attention. But immediately after this he went into one of his best film performances ever, as Mr Dorrit in Christine Edzard's two-part version of Dickens's *Little Dorrit*. An interesting scripting decision makes the two parts not consecutive, but interlocking, presenting two aspects of the same story. The first is through the appalled eyes of Arthur Clennam, an outsider who perceives the Dorrits' world as dark and horrible, while in the second everything is illuminated by Little Dorrit's own sunny and innocent perceptions. Guinness, as the heroine's monstrously selfish, self-absorbed father, comes into his own in the second half, climaxing in his agonizingly public break-down and leisurely Dickensian deathbed scene. Guinness was delighted with the approach of the adaptor/director, who encouraged improvisation and in particular let the deathbed scene go on and on until he was convinced (wrongly as it proved) that it would be pruned down from its high-Victorian luxuriance before the public saw it. The performance is brilliant, and yet again one can but wonder at Guinness's readiness to play a truly odious figure without ever tipping even half a wink that this is a nice, lovable actor just pretending to be nasty.

ABOVE: As Shylock in Chichester Festival Theatre's production of The Merchant of Venice.

Quite coincidentally, the Dickens connection persisted in Guinness's next film, *A Handful of Dust* (1988), in which he played the gentle but inescapable tyrant into whose hands Evelyn Waugh's hapless hero finally falls. The only pleasure left to Mr Todd, exiled in the jungle far from civilisation, is to be read to endlessly by his guest, and what better to keep them both occupied, year after year, than the collected works of Charles Dickens? By this time Guinness felt that it was also time to return to the West End stage, and found a suitable vehicle in an American two-character piece, Lee Blessing's *A Walk in the Woods*. It is a simple piece – perhaps simple to the point of naïvety – about a meeting between two arms negotiators, the older Russian, ironical and elusive, the younger American, deadly serious and earnest. As they circle warily and it becomes more and more evident that their respective masters do not intend them to progress very far (for this is still in the midst of the Cold War), the cliches tend to pile up, but in a way the very thinness of the text provides an opportunity for the actors to fill out their characters with telling business and human observation. Another character that Guinness could play with both hands tied behind his back, the Russian still called forth a mesmerising display of sheer skill and unquestionable stage presence.

As he approached eighty, it seemed only natural that Guinness should relax a bit. After *A Handful of Dust* and *A Walk in the Woods* he made few significant appearances. In 1991 he went to Prague to play a small, very mysterious and 'Kafkaesque' role as the Chief Clerk in Steven Soderbergh's odd but effective thriller *Kafka*, a fictional addition to the known facts of the writer's life. Much more significant was a dazzling demonstration of his old skill at making the most out of an image of silent suffering, the humility which takes humiliation as a heaven-sent trial which one would not dream of questioning or railing against. The occasion this time was a television film of Christopher Hampton's play *Tales from Hollywood*, which supposes for the sake of argument that the Hungarian-German playwright Ödön von Horváth, instead of being killed by lightning in Paris in 1938, survived and went to Hollywood, like so many other émigré German writers. There his life impinges on those of some of the most famous, such as Brecht, Thomas Mann and his (in English-speaking countries at least) much less well-known brother Heinrich, author of the novel on which *The Blue Angel* was based. While Thomas Mann was rich and successful in America, Heinrich was really down on his luck, and in addition had to cope with the excesses of what all his friends and relatives considered a most unsuitable wife, a good-hearted but hopelessly improvident and promiscuous ex-barmaid who seemed sometimes helplessly driven to humiliate him in public. Bearded as in his previous incarnations of Freud, Guinness gave an intense and deeply moving performance, which has been called by Benedict Nightingale 'quintessential Guinness, deft and detailed yet sentient and profound'; as with Smiley in his marital problems, the less he asked for or even tolerated sympathy, the more you felt for him.

Never one to rest on his laurels, even after a performance like that, widely recognised as among the finest in the annals of television, Guinness next launched out on something totally new for him, though as he insisted the realisation of a long-felt ambition. 'I've always admired the Buster Keaton movies and long to have a stab at it. Well, all right, this isn't that, but it's as near as I could get, in a way.' The point is that in his screenplay for *A Foreign Field*, specially written for Guinness, Roy Clarke has given the character a sum total of five words. Amos, a Second World War soldier visiting the scene of the Normandy landings with his old mate Cyril (Leo McKern) has been left by his injuries with the mind of an eight-year-old, and has virtually nothing to say for himself in this serio-comic walk down memory lane. Extraordinary role, one would think, to give a man whose forte had always been playing people of sharp and devious intelligence, as well as being in private life one of the most articulate of men. But Guinness was always, as well, an accomplished mime and one of the most subtle of physical actors, so the role held few problems for him and, even wordless, he dominates the film. His own verdict? 'You see the film and realize what you did wrong. I don't think I've done anything that's good, but I've been in some good things.'

Advancing into his eighties Alec Guinness was still a big star, still a formidable actor, able to choose exactly what he wanted to do, in any medium, a law unto himself, and quite unlike anyone else. He chose to make what proved to be his last appearance in Jack Rosenthal's television script *Eskimo Day* (1996), which called again for an exercise in emotional restraint, with everything buried. And still, for all we knew of him, all the many faces he had assumed behind which we thought we glimpsed the one real face, he remained deeply mysterious. Genuinely modest, genuinely retiring and concerned with preserving his own privacy, he yet in a curious way allowed himself, in Arthur Miller's phrase, to be totally known. In his last five years he chose to write more than he acted, producing two further volumes which were sort of autobiographical, in a typically elusive way, being based on the diaries he kept during his virtual retirement. Neither *My Name Escapes Me* (1996) nor *A Positively Final Appearance* (1999), though quirkily personal in tone, finally took us much closer to the man himself.

Guinness was, in the truest sense, a sphinx without a secret: we just thought he had a secret because we would not believe the answer to acting genius could be so simple. And the answer, simple as it is, was not complete: not because Guinness himself complicated matters, but because his kind of talent is finally something given, not made – the wind bloweth where it listeth, and sometimes, all unpredictably, a lonely child given to fantasizing his situation proves able to involve the whole world in his fantasy. And what of the man himself? What made him happy? His family, his religion, work, and the ability to keep on working, and, well, life: 'It's on a summer weekend in Hampshire with agreeable guests, sitting around on the patio for lunch and then dinner with a game of croquet in between somewhere. Come dark on a warm night – to make it all sound grander – it's listening to music, star-gazing, sipping something. It's Beethoven's last sonata perhaps. No, these days it will be Haydn. He's so kind of sane that it makes one feel sane, however mad one is – and happy.'

174

OPPOSITE: An informal portrait of Sir Alec by Snowdon.

OVERLEAF: Another Oscar, this time in 1980, for a lifetime's service.

AFTERGLOW

hen I was writing the first version of this biography, my relations with Guinness were – characteristically, I suppose I should say – perverse and contradictory. The occasion was his seventieth birthday, which took place in 1984. Now I had got to know Guinness quite well, on a professional level, when I was Film Critic of *The Times* in the Sixties, and had continued in close touch with him when I returned from teaching in Los Angeles in 1978. So when the idea came up of my writing a celebratory biography – the first, as it happened – I naturally wrote to him immediately asking if he would talk to me in connection with the proposed book. This was, I might add, just weeks after I had done a lengthy interview with him of which he had told me explicitly he approved. So I did not expect any particular problem, apart from, probably, some difficulties of time and location. His answer, therefore, rather took me by surprise. He wrote back, with the extreme courtesy which characterised all his dealings with people, to say that of course he had no doubts of my

PREVIOUS PAGE: Guinness at the BAFTA Awards in 1989, after being awarded the Fellowship of the British Academy, the highest honour in acting.

LEFT: Guinness in London during his later years.

ABOVE: Alec Guinness relaxes outside on the veranda.

probity, responsibility, accuracy and all of that, but he did not feel that he could see me at that point because he was then engaged on writing a book which 'my publishers, though not of course I, regard as an autobiography'.

Over-scrupulous? Or merely calculating on the possible limits of my gentlemanliness (or his own) if it came down to who would get to use first any story which my probing might elicit from his carefully stimulated memory? I could not begin to guess, but I knew him well enough to accept his ruling without demur: he could, after all, for all his insistence on his own uncertainties, be very stubborn if challenged on a decision, especially one which seemed to involve a matter of principle. So I took the only course which seemed open to me, and went ahead with the book – which was never supposed to be any sort of official, authorised biography – on the same basis that I would if the subject were dead or otherwise seriously inaccessible. That is, I talked to everyone I could think of that had ever worked with or known Guinness, ransacked the files, dug into my own memories.

LEFT: *Alec Guinness and Lauren Bacall star in the television movie,* A Foreign Field. *Guinness plays a D-Day war veteran who was wounded on the battlefield leaving him with the intelligence of an 8-year-old boy.*

So far, so good. The book came out on time for the anniversary, and was, if I say it myself, quite gratifyingly received. Some six months went by, and then I began to get what I took to be coded messages from Guinness, by way of at least three mutual friends. Alec, they said, is very distressed, because your book is riddled with errors. Taking the bull by the horns, I tackled Guinness directly, saying that I was distressed that he was distressed, and wondering if he would care to let me know what these errors were. Immediately he invited me to lunch – at the Connaught, apparently his favourite restaurant in London. And once we were ensconced (I took great care to be a couple of minutes before time, knowing that lateness was one thing he could not stomach) he touched off immediately, in confessional mode. He blamed himself, of course. Yes, it would have been much more sensible if he had agreed to talk with me at once. But, well, really he had hoped that if he would not cooperate I would not write the book. Not that he had anything against such a book being written by me specifically – perish the thought. He had just vaguely hoped that no one would ever be moved to write a biography of him. 'But, I suppose one has to accept...'

So what about the errors? As it turned out the only actual error he could pinpoint was that a minor figure in one of the pictures of a pre-war stage production was wrongly identified in the caption. Fair enough: it was my mistake to believe without question what the caption the picture came with said. And...? He began to look slightly uncomfortable. Well, it was not important, but he thought he might perhaps mention that the construction I had put on what little evidence I then had on the details of his birth was 'arguable'. I reassured him (or possibly alarmed him) immediately that since originally writing the book I had managed to run to earth his birth certificate, through finding his marriage certificate and tracing back. Actually I privately thought that it tended to confirm my first hypothesis: I had suggested in the book that his mother might possibly have been a servant in his father's respectable Marylebone household. Oh no, said Guinness; he had in fact resulted from an indiscretion during Cowes Week, 1913. I definitely had the feeling from the way this was put that he was rebuking me for assigning his mother an unduly humble place in society; he went on quite cheerfully to tell me that the date of conception was important, as in his childhood bastards conceived prewar had the edge socially on wartime babies. Wasn't that odd?, I said; after all the idea of a child conceived on the eve of a serviceman's departure for the front seemed rather grand and romantic. To us, yes, said Guinness; but then as now, children are beastly unromantic creatures. He gave me one of his benign, mysterious smiles, and went on inconsequentially to rubbish the suggestion in Omar Sharif's autobiography that he had finally found peace by returning to 'the faith of his childhood', Judaism. 'Why, I'm not even circumcised.'

I tell this story at some length because I think it throws a lot of light on the enigmatic character of Guinness. At every stage his behaviour is devious. He did not tell me directly that he did not want a biography written: a wish that I would quite probably have respected. He did not tell me himself that he had read my book and was worried by its errors – which proved anyway to be a mere pretext. He did not flatly contradict me in my reading of his mother's circumstances at the time he was conceived, suggesting instead that he was not quite sure himself, but thought my idea was arguable. He, I think deliberately, let me suppose that his version of things was intended unequivocally to move his mother several notches up the social register. He knew that I was then preparing a revision and updating of the book for an impending paperback edition, and clearly wanted me to incorporate his 'corrections' in the new version. Which, of course, I duly did.

One interesting thing to me is that subsequent to our lunch (and the death of his mother), Guinness felt himself able to go into more detail about his conception – from which it emerged that his placing of the event in Cowes Week, far from moving his mother up the social scale, really moved her down. She was certainly not there, as he had allowed one to infer, as the sort of society lady who naturally would be there, nor yet as a respectable but fallible nursemaid, but instead as a waitress/barmaid on the Guinness family yacht, and even possibly something of a call-girl. But then, is that unequivocally true, or merely an expression of that masochistic streak which often seemed to be present in Guinness's psyche, a desire to present himself and his origins in the worst possible light, as though that will somehow assuage his inborn sense of guilt? Also, the haziness of the details seems to be partially an enjoyment, or perhaps a deep psychological need, on Guinness's part to preserve and foster a sense of mystery about himself. It may be noted that though, in his late autobiographical (well, sort of autobiographical) volumes he goes on rather about his interest in definitely identifying his father, even his need to do so, it must occur to the most casual reader that he wilfully does not follow up obvious leads, as though he does not really, in his heart of hearts, want to know. (Even the blood tests which, we are told, proved that definitely he was not a Guinness were initiated, not by him, but by an interested member of the Guinness family.)

My last communication with him was, coincidentally, concerned with his parentage. In Dublin I had noticed that just round the corner from the Guinness distillery was a De Cuffe Street, just the form of name his mother had adopted from her original, simpler 'Cuffe', and wrote to him to wonder whether there might not be a Guinness connection on his mother's side rather than, as had always been assumed, on his father's. Interesting possibility, he replied vaguely; I must look into it. But needless to say, he never did.

So what does all this have to do with Guinness's star persona, and his relationship with his public? I think it all refers back, and gives context to, the deep-buried sense of hurt which underlies everything he did. All those reminiscing about Guinness seemed to come back, with relish not unmixed with irritation, to the contradictions in his character. Gielgud was famed for the extraordinary number of bricks he dropped in everyday life – so many that people often wondered whether most of it was deliberate, a defence possibly, or a stratagem for making character. Generally his obituarists enjoyed their stories, and found them lovable. And the same, mutatis mutandis, seems to apply to Guinness. However maddening his eccentricities might sometimes be, they always seem to have occasioned affection. Christopher Sinclair-Stevenson, the editor who managed to extract *Blessings in Disguise* from him, recollected in *The Times* that when Guinness had completed the first draft he was peculiarly elusive.

BELOW: *Alec Guinness's biographies (from left to right):* My Name Escapes Me *(1996);* Blessings in Disguise *(1985); and* A Positively Final Appearance *(1999).*

RIGHT: Guinness as Amos in the television movie, A Foreign Field *(only his third television performance).*

Arranging a lunch at which he would, just possibly, hand over the manuscript, he professed to be worried: 'But isn't that rather a long way from your office? I have a parcel to give you, and it may be too much of a nuisance to carry back.' Sinclair-Stevenson did not even know for sure what the parcel was to contain, but proved to have guessed right: after lunch Guinness handed over the parcel with, 'If you don't think it's any good, and I am not at all sure that it is, just say so. I won't show it to any other publisher. I'll just put it away.' Was he sincere in all this diffidence? Sinclair-Stevenson thought he was, and loved him for it.

Then we have to remember that many of Guinness's greatest triumphs were in comedy, especially from Ealing, and there is no doubt that the effect of a number of his more dramatic roles depended importantly on a highly developed sense of the ridiculous, how to play on it, counteract it, evade it. Humour is generally, if not quite always, lovable, and there were many testimonies after Guinness's death to his charm as a conversationalist and his comic edge as an actor. And, of course, to his tremendous modesty. Sometimes there was hint that it could be infuriating, because so neurotically exaggerated. But as *The Times* pointed out, he could certainly see the funny side of it himself: he liked to tell the story of an occasion when he handed his coat to a hotel cloakroom and was about to give his name when he was told it was not necessary. He was rather pleased at this basic evidence of his fame, until he came back to pick it up and noticed that the attached ticket said simply, 'Bald with glasses'.

The really big story which turned up one way and another in all the obituaries was that Guinness had been made a millionaire by *Star Wars*, but professed to hate the film. This also seemed to have something to do with his modesty – or was it his snobbery? At the time of making he had said, reasonably (or at least tactfully) enough, that he liked it because, though he had some reservations about the quality of the dialogue and claimed never to have quite understood who or what he was playing, he saw it as a universal fairy-story, well told, with a hopeful message for the times. But by the end of the Nineties his opinion had markedly changed. He was thoroughly fed up with being accosted everywhere with enthusiastic cries of 'May the force be with you!', and seemed somehow to mistrust, or find distasteful, the sheer appalling popularity of it all. But he was not, after all, entirely averse to the money it brought him in his old age. John Mortimer recollected encountering him in the gents of a London club and admiring his jacket. 'Feel it,' he said; 'What do you think it's made of?' It was very soft, and Mortimer guessed cashmere. '"No", his voice rumbled, deeply amused; "Mink." I'm still not sure if he was joking.'

He was a funny man. He was a tortured man. He was a man who derived his humour from his own traumas, and achieved, on the surface at least, a philosophical calm which reassured him, and those who observed it, without seeming in any way preachy or priggish. He could play a monster. But he could play a truly good man, which is much more difficult. People loved him as either, because they always sensed that whatever effect he achieved was hard-won. You could not see the wheels going round, but you knew they were there, and like the mills of God, they ground very small.

CHRONOLOGY · ALEC GUINNESS · STAGE, FILM, TV

THEATRE/FILM/TV	TITLE	AUTHOR	ROLE	DIRECTOR
1933				
Film	*Evensong*	Edward Knoblock, Dorothy Farnum	Extra	Victor Saville
1934				
Playhouse	*Libel!*	Edward Wooll	Junior Counsel	Leon M. Lion
Piccadilly	*Queer Cargo*	Noel Langley	Chinese coolie, French pirate, English sailor	Reginald Back
New	*Hamlet*	Shakespeare	Osric, Third Player	John Gielgud
1935				
New	*Noah*	André Obey	Wolf	Michel Saint-Denis
New	*Romeo and Juliet*	Shakespeare	Sampson, Apothecary	John Gielgud
1936				
New	*The Seagull*	Anton Chekhov	Workman, then Yakov	Theodore Komisarjevsky
1936–37				
Old Vic	*Love's Labour's Lost*	Shakespeare	Boyet	Tyrone Guthrie
Old Vic	*As You Like It*	Shakespeare	Le Beau, William	Tyrone Guthrie
Old Vic	*The Witch of Edmonton*	William Rowley, Thomas Dekker, John Ford	Old Thorney	Michel Saint-Denis
Old Vic	*Hamlet*	Shakespeare	Osric, Reynaldo	Tyrone Guthrie
Old Vic	*Twelfth Night*	Shakespeare	Sir Andrew Aguecheek	Tyrone Guthrie
Old Vic	*Henry V*	Shakespeare	Exeter	Tyrone Guthrie
Elsinore	*Hamlet*	Shakespeare	Osric, Player Queen, Renaldo	Tyrone Guthrie
1937–38				
Queen's	*Richard II*	Shakespeare	Aumerle, Groom	John Gielgud
Queen's	*The School for Scandal*	Sheridan	Snake	Tyrone Guthrie
Queen's	*The Three Sisters*	Chekhov	Fedotik	Michel Saint-Denis
Queen's	*The Merchant of Venice*	Shakespeare	Lorenzo	John Gielgud
Richmond	*The Doctor's Dilemma*	George Bernard Shaw	Louis Dubedat	Bernard Miles
Old Vic	*Trelawny of the 'Wells'*	Arthur Wing Pinero	Arthur Gower	Tyrone Guthrie
Old Vic	*Hamlet*	Shakespeare	Hamlet	Tyrone Guthrie
Old Vic	*The Rivals*	Sheridan	Bob Acres	Esme Church
1939				
Tour Europe and Egypt	*Hamlet*	Shakespeare	Hamlet	Tyrone Guthrie

THEATRE/FILM/TV	TITLE	AUTHOR	ROLE	DIRECTOR
Tour	*Henry V*	Shakespeare	Chorus	Tyrone Guthrie
Tour	*The Rivals*	Sheridan	Bob Acres	Tyrone Guthrie
Tour	*Libel!*	Edward Wooll	Emile Flordon	Leon M. Lion
Old Vic	*The Ascent of F6*	W. H. Auden, Christopher Isherwood	Michael Ransom	Rupert Doone
Perth	*Romeo and Juliet*	Shakespeare	Romeo	William Stoker
Rudolf Steiner Hall	*Great Expectations*	Alec Guinness	Herbert Pocket	George Devine
1940				
Globe	*Cousin Muriel*	Clemence Dane	Richard Meilhac	Normal Marshall
Old Vic	*The Tempest*	Shakespeare	Ferdinand	George Devine, Marius Goring
English tour	*Thunder Rock*	Robert Ardrey	Charleston	Herbert Marshall
1942				
Henry Miller, New York	*Flare Path*	Terence Rattigan	Fl. Lt. Graham	Margaret Webster
1945				
Albert Hall	*Heart of Oak* (pageant)	Edward Neil	Nelson	S. Albert Locke
1946				
Lyric	*The Brothers Karamazov*	Chekhov	Mitya	Peter Brook
Arts	*Vicious Circle* (Huis Clos)	Jean-Paul Sartre	Garcin	Peter Brook
Film	*Great Expectations*	Ronald Neame	Herbert Pocket	David Lean
1946–47				
New	*King Lear*	Shakespeare	Fool	Laurence Olivier
New	*An Inspector Calls*	J. B. Priestley	Eric Birling	Basil Dean
New	*Cyrano de Bergerac*	Edmond Rostand	De Guiche	Tyrone Guthrie
New	*The Alchemist*	Ben Jonson	Abel Drugger	John Burrell
1947–48				
New	*Richard II*	Shakespeare	Richard II	Ralph Richardson
New	*Saint Joan*	George Bernard Shaw	The Dauphin	John Burrell
New	*The Government Inspector*	Gogol	Hlestakov	John Burrell
New	*Coriolanus*	Shakespeare	Menenius Agrippa	E. Martin Browne
New	*Twelfth Night*	Shakespeare	–	Alec Guinness
Film	*Oliver Twist*	David Lean	Fagin	David Lean
1949				
Savoy	*The Human Touch*	J. Lee Thompson, Dudley Leslie	Dr James Simpson	Peter Ashmore
Lyceum, Edinburgh	*The Cocktail Party*	T. S. Eliot	Sir Henry Harcourt-Reilly	E. Martin Browne
Film	*Kind Hearts and Coronets*	Robert Hamer, John Dighton	The d' Ascoyne family	Robert Hamer
Film	*A Run for Your Money*	Richard Hughes	Whimple	Charles Frend

Theatre/Film/TV	Title	Author	Role	Director
1950				
Henry Miller, New York	*The Cocktail Party*	T. S. Eliot	Sir Henry Harcourt-Reilly	E. Martin Browne
Film	*Last Holiday*	J. B. Priestley	George Bird	Henry Cass
Film	*The Mudlark*	Nunnally Johnson	Disraeli	Jean Negulesco
1951				
New	*Hamlet*	Shakespeare	Hamlet	Alec Guinness, Frank Hauser
Film	*The Lavender Hill Mob*	T. E. B. Clarke	Henry Holland	Charles Crichton
Film	*The Man in the White Suit*	John Dighton, Alexander Mackendrick, Roger MacDougall	Sidney Stratton	Alexander Mackendrick
1952				
Aldwych	*Under the Sycamore Tree*	Sam and Bella Spewack	The Ant Scientist	Peter Glenville
Film	*The Card*	Eric Ambler	Denry Machin	Ronald Neame
1953				
Shakespeare Playhouse, Stratford, Ontario	*All's Well That Ends Well*	Shakespeare	King of France	Tyrone Guthrie
Shakespeare Playhouse, Stratford, Ontario	*Richard III*	Shakespeare	Richard III	Tyrone Guthrie
Film	*Malta Story*	William Fairchild, Nigel Balchin	Flight Lieutenant Peter Ross	Brian Desmond Hurst
Film	*Father Brown*	Thelma Schnee, Robert Hamer	Father Brown	Robert Hamer
1954				
Globe	*The Prisoner*	Bridget Boland	The Cardinal	Peter Glenville
Documentary Film	*The Stratford Adventure*	Gudrun Parker	Himself	Morten Parker
1955				
Film	*To Paris with Love*	Robert Hamer	Col. Sir Edgar Fraser	Robert Hamer
Film	*The Prisoner*	Bridget Boland	The Cardinal	Peter Glenville
Film	*The Ladykillers*	William Rose	Professor Marcus	Alexander Mackendrick
Documentary Film	*Rowlandson's England*	John Hawkesworth, Robert Hamer	Narrator	John Hawkesworth
1956				
Winter Garden	*Hotel Paradiso*	Georges Feydeau, Maurice Desvallieres	Boniface	Peter Glenville
Film	*The Swan*	John Dighton	Prince Albert	Charles Vidor

Theatre/Film/TV	Title	Author	Role	Director
1957				
Film	*The Bridge on the River Kwai*	Pierre Boule, Carl Foreman	Colonel Nicholson	David Lean
Film	*Barnacle Bill*	T.E.B.Clarke	William Horatio Ambrose	Charles Frend
1958				
Film	*The Horse's Mouth*	Alec Guinness	Gulley Jimson	Ronald Neame
1959				
	The Scapegoat	Robert Hamer, Gore Vidal	John Barrett, Jacques de Gue	Robert Hamer
TV	*The Wicked Scheme of Jebel Deeks*	John D. Hess	Jebel Deeks	Franklin Shaffner
1960				
Haymarket	*Ross*	Terence Rattigan	T.E. Lawrence	Glen Byam Shaw
Film	*Our Man in Havana*	Graham Greene	Jim Wormold	Carol Reed
Film	*Tunes of Glory*	James Kennaway	Lieut.Col. Jock Sinclair	Ronald Neame
1961				
Film	*Majority of One*	Leonard Spigelgass	Koichi Asano	Mervyn LeRoy
1962				
Film	*HMS Defiant*	Nigel Kneale	Captain Crawford	Lewis Gilbert
Film	*Lawrence of Arabia*	Robert Bolt	Prince Feisul	David Lean
1963				
Lyceum, Edinburgh	*Exit the King*	Eugene Ionesco	Berenger	George Devine
1964				
Plymouth, New York	*Dylan*	Sidney Michaels	Dylan Thomas	
Film	*The Fall of the Roman Empire*	Ben Barzman, Philip Yordan	Marcus Aurelius	Anthony Mann
1965				
Film	*Situation Hopeless – But Not Serious*	Silvia Reinhardt	Herr Frick	Gottfried Reinhardt
Film	*Doctor Zhivago*	Robert Bolt	General Yegraf Zhivago	David Lean
1966				
Phoenix	*Incident at Vichy*	Arthur Miller	Von Berg	Peter Wood
Royal Court	*Macbeth*	Shakespeare	Macbeth	William Gaskell
Film	*Hotel Paradiso*	Peter Glenville, Jean-Claude Carrière	Boniface	Peter Glenville
Film	*The Quiller Memorandum*	Harold Pinter	Pol	Michael Anderson

Theatre/Film/TV	Title	Author	Role	Director
1967				
Wyndham's	*Wise Child*	Simon Gray	Mrs Artminster	John Dexter
Film	*The Comedians*	Graham Greene	Major Jones	Peter Glenville
1968				
Chichester Festival Theatre, Wyndham's, Haymarket	*The Cocktail Party*	T.S.Eliot	Sir Henry Harcourt-Reilly	Alec Guinness
1969				
TV	*Conversation at Night*	Friedrich Dürrenmatt	Executioner	Rudolf Cartier
1970				
Yvonne Arnaud, Guildford	*Time Out of Mind*	Bridget Boland	John	Stephen Barry
Film	*Cromwell*	Ken Hughes	Charles I	Ken Hughes
Film	*Scrooge*	Leslie Bricusse	Marley's Ghost	Ronald Neame
TV	*Twelfth Night*	Shakespeare	Malvolio	John Dexter, John Sichel
1971				
Haymarket	*A Voyage Round My Father*	John Mortimer	Father	Ronald Eyre
1972				
TV	*Solo*	e. e. cummings	–	James Cellan Jones
1973				
Lyric	*Habeas Corpus*	Alan Bennett	Dr Wicksteed	Ronald Eyre
Film	*Brother Sun, Sister Moon*	Franco Zeffirelli, Lina Wertmuller, Kenneth Ross	The Pope	Franco Zeffirelli
Film	*Hitler – The Last Ten Days*	Ennio de Concini, Maria Fusco, Ivan Moffat	Adolf Hitler	Ennio de Concini
1974				
TV	*The Gift of Friendship*	John Osborne	Jocelyn Broome	Mike Newell
TV	*Caesar and Cleopatra*	George Bernard Shaw	Julius Caesar	James Cellan Jones
1975				
Apollo	*A Family and a Fortune*	Julian Mitchell	Dudley	Alan Strachan
1976				
Queen's	*Yahoo*	Alec Guinness, Alan Strachan	Dean Swift	Alan Strachan
Film	*Murder by Death*	Neil Simon	Bensonmum	Robert Moore
1977				
Queen's	*The Old Country*	Alan Bennett	Hilary	Clifford Williams
Film	*Star Wars*	George Lucas	Obi-Ben Kenobi	George Lucas
1979				
TV	*Tinker, Tailor, Soldier, Spy*	Arthur Hopcraft	George Smiley	John Irvin

Theatre/Film/TV	Title	Author	Role	Director
1980				
Film	*The Empire Strikes Back*	Leigh Brackett, Lawrence Kasdan	Obi-Ben Kenobi	Irvin Kershner
Film	*Raise the Titanic*	Adam Kennedy	Bigalow	Jerry Jameson
Film	*Little Lord Fauntleroy*	Blanche Hanalis	Earl of Dorincourt	Jack Gold
1981				
TV	*Smiley's People*	John Hopkins, John Le Carré	George Smiley	Simon Langton
1982				
Film	*Lovesick*	Marshall Brickman	Sigmund Freud	Marshall Brickman
1983				
Film	*Return of the Jedi*	Lawrence Kasdan, George Lucas	Obi-Ben Kenobi	Richard Marquand
Film (released 1995)	*Silent Witness*	Anthony Waller	"Mystery guest star"	Anthony Waller
1984				
Film	*A Passage to India*	David Lean	Professor Godbole	David Lean
Chichester Festival Theatre	*The Merchant of Venice*	Shakespeare	Shylock	–
1985				
TV Film	*Monsignor Quixote*	Christopher Neame	Father Quixote	Rodney Bennett
1987				
Film	*Little Dorrit*	Christine Edzard	Mr Dorrit	Christine Edzard
1988				
Film	*A Handful of Dust*	Tim Sullivan, Derek Granger, Charles Sturridge	Mr Todd	Charles Sturridge
Comedy Theatre	*A Walk in the Woods*	Lee Blessing	Andrey Botvinnik	Ronald Eyre
1991				
Film	*Kafka*	Lem Dobbs	The Chief Clerk	Steven Soderbergh
1992				
TV Film	*Tales from Hollywood*	Christopher Hampton	Heinrich Mann	Howard Davies
1993				
TV Film	*A Foreign Field*	Roy Clarke	Amos	Charles Sturridge
1996				
TV Film	*Eskimo Day*	Jack Rosenthal	Father	Piers Haggard
Radio	*My Name Escapes Me*	Alec Guinness	Reader	

BIBLIOGRAPHY

BOOKS

Bette Davis: *The Lonely Life*, (New York) 1962

Ronald Harwood (ed): *Dear Alec: Guinness at 75*, (London) 1989

Allan Hunter: *Alec Guinness on Screen*, (Edinburgh) 1982

Viola Meynell (ed.): *The Best of Friends*, Letters to Sir Sydney Cockerell, (London) 1956

Garry O'Connor: *Alec Guinness: Master of Disguise*, (London) 1994

Michael Parkinson: *The Best of Parkinson*, (London) 1982

Graham Payn, Sheridan Morley (eds.): *The Noël Coward Diaries*, (London) 1982

Kenneth Tynan: *Alec Guinness*, (London) 1953

WRITINGS BY GUINNESS

'I took my landing craft to the Sicily Beaches', *Daily Telegraph*, 20 August, 1943

'Money for Jam', *The Penguin New Writing, No. 26,* 1945

'My Idea of Hamlet', *The Spectator*, 6 July, 1951

'The "Horse" and I', *The Observer,* 1 February, 1959

'Cakes and Ale No More', *The Spectator,* 22 October, 1983

Blessings in Disguise, (London) 1985

My Name Escapes Me: The Diary of a Retiring Actor, (London) 1996

A Positively Final Appearance, (London) 1999

INTERVIEWS

Anon: 'Least Likely to Succeed', *Time*, 21 April, 1958

Terry Coleman: 'The Still of the Knight', *The Guardian*, 19 May, 1973

Sydney Edwards: 'Dishonest Englishmen', *Evening Standard*, 10 September, 1976

Terence Feely: 'Nothing But the Truth: Sir Alec Guinness', *Sunday Graphic*, 26 July, 1959

Richard Findlater: 'Guinness: Behind the Mask', *The Observer*, 9 December 1984

James Green: 'London's Pride, I: Sir Alec Guinness', *Evening News*, 5 February, 1968

Ronald Hayman: 'Alec Guinness', *The Times,* 7 August, 1971

John Higgins: 'Star Talk about Star Wars', *The Times*, 8 December, 1977

Richard Last: 'Guinness and the Garrulous Dictator', *Daily Telegraph*, 9 December, 1974

Roderick Mann: 'Ambitions? At Fifty I have none left, says Guinness', *Sunday Express*, 7 May, 1964

Sheridan Morley: 'A Swift Look at Alec Guinness', *The Times*, 4 October, 1976

Tim Satchell: 'Meeting People: How Sir Alec found the name of a begging letter writer', *Sunday Express*, 19 February, 1977

Tom Sutcliffe: 'A Secret Surface', *The Guardian*, 8 September, 1979

John Russell Taylor: 'Alec Guinness', *American Film*, April, 1989

Nicholas Wapshott: 'The Times Profile: Sir Alec Guinness: Smiley Looks Back', *The Times*, 30 November, 1981

PHOTOGRAPHIC ACKNOWLEDGEMENTS

The publisher has endeavoured to acknowledge all copyright holders of the pictures reproduced in this book. However, in view of the complexity of securing copyright information, should any photographs not be correctly attributed, then the publisher undertakes to make any appropriate changes in future editions of this book.

BBC Copyright Photographs: 150, 157, 164, 165; Cecil Beaton Archive at Sothebys: 71; Camera Press: 6, 51, 183, 177, 179; Chichester Festival Theatre: 170 (bottom); Donald Cooper: 145, 147, 163; Zoë Dominic: 126, 142; Clive Francis: 1; Globe Theatre (H.M. Tenents): 34 (right); Hirschfeld: 129 (left); Kobal Collection: 19, 49, 58, 59 (top & bottom left), 63, 68, 69, 79, 80, 84 (bottom), 87, 94 (bottom), 102, 103, 106, 107 (top), 109, 113, 115 (bottom), 119, 121, 124, 125, 131, 137, 140, 141, 144, 146 (bottom), 148, 154, 159, 160, 161; Raymond Mander & Joe Mitchenson Collection: 9, 14 (top & bottom right), 21 (bottom). 22 (top left), 23, 29 (right), 30, 42, 66 (left); Angus McBean: 2, 28, 34 (left), 35, 43, 88, 116, 117, 143; Moviestore Collection: 180; National Film Archive: 65, 83, 90, 91, 92, 95 (top), 123 (bottom left & right), 136, 149,167, 169 (right); National Portrait Gallery (Howard Coster): 17; Popperfoto: 89, 96, 104, 105, 134, 135, 138, 139, 173; Punch Magazine: 24 (bottom right), 38, 61, 84 (top), 112, 146 (top right), 152 (bottom); Radio Times Hulton Picture Library: 27, 33, 36, 48, 53 (top left), 56, 57, 59 (bottom right) 67, 72, 82, 101, 107 (bottom), 114, 123 (top), 127 (right); Rex Features: 97, 108, 110, 118, 128, 129 (right), 178, 130, 146 (top left), 152 (top); Ronald Searle: 66 (right), 80; Stratford Festival Archives, Ontario: 85, 86; Theatre Museum, Victoria & Albert Museum: 14 (bottom left), 21 (top), 22 (bottom left), 24 (top & bottom left), 25, 26 (bottom), 30 (top left), 31, 45 (John Vickers), 64, 81, 95 (bottom) 127 (left), 155; Thorn/EMI Screen Entertainment: 170 (top); John Timbers: 143, 168; Time Inc., 1958: 99; Topham Picture Library: 115 (top); Van Damm Collection, New York Public Library: 37; John Vickers: 44 (left), 46, 47, 53 (top right & bottom), 54, 55.

The publishers greatly appreciate the assistance and co-operation given by Sheila Formoy at H.M. Tennents and the staff at the Richmond Reference Library.